SUPERINVESTORS

Every owner of a physical copy of this edition of

SUPERINVESTORS

can download the eBook for free direct from us at Harriman House, in a DRM-free format that can be read on any eReader, tablet or smartphone.

Simply head to:

EBOOKS.HARRIMAN-HOUSE.COM/SUPERINVESTORS

to get your copy now.

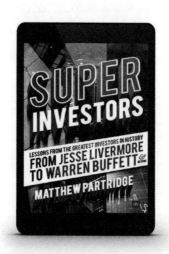

SUPERINVESTORS

Lessons from the greatest investors in history

━━━

From Jesse Livermore to
Warren Buffett & beyond

Matthew Partridge

Hh Harriman House

HARRIMAN HOUSE LTD
18 College Street
Petersfield
Hampshire
GU31 4AD
GREAT BRITAIN
Tel: +44 (0)1730 233870

Email: enquiries@harriman-house.com
Website: www.harriman-house.com

First published in Great Britain in 2017.
Copyright © Matthew Partridge

The right of Matthew Partridge to be identified as the author has been asserted in accordance with the Copyright, Design and Patents Act 1988.

Paperback ISBN: 978-0-85719-597-5
eBook ISBN: 978-0-85719-598-2

British Library Cataloguing in Publication Data
A CIP catalogue record for this book can be obtained from the British Library.

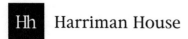

To Bernadette and Tony, my wonderful parents,
for all their support over the years.

CONTENTS

ABOUT THE AUTHOR

Matthew Partridge is an experienced financial journalist. He writes for *MoneyWeek* magazine, Britain's biggest-selling personal finance weekly. A trained historian, Matthew did a degree in economics and history at the University of Durham, before doing a master's and a doctorate in economic history at the London School of Economics. He has taught at Goldsmiths, University of London, as well as spending time at various investment banks and a well-known economics consultancy.

FOREWORD
by Clive Moffatt

I T H A S O F T E N been said that the stock market is a discounter of all known information – so what is the point of this new book by Matthew Partridge? Well, it is fun for a start. He investigates and rates the performance and impact of 20 'superinvestors' spanning the last 200 years. If you are a private investor it will show you what can make for success. If you are a professional fund manager it will provide you with useful insights on your rivals and those who came before you – and perhaps get you rating yourself.

The investment market has been transformed in scope and complexity since David Ricardo (who you will meet in chapter 2) speculated successfully on the outcome of the Battle of Waterloo but, according to Matthew, success still requires knowledge, an appetite for risk, good timing and luck. As in other areas of life, it is just as much an art as it is a science.

Since the 2008 global financial meltdown, people have become sceptical about professional fund managers. Matthew captures the mood in a few apt words: "the overall message seems to be that it's difficult to beat the market over the long run and that most investment professionals are nothing more than highly paid coin-flippers".

On the other hand, ultra-low interest rates since 2008 have made it very clear that no one is going to get rich – nor are pension funds going to be able to meet their targets – by simply putting cash in savings accounts. And with cheap money, stock markets have recovered significantly. The challenge facing investors is how to secure an above-average return in rapidly changing global markets.

To that end, Matthew turns the spotlight on a variety of mostly professional investors from past and present, ranging from David Ricardo and Benjamin Graham to Warren Buffett and Neil Woodford. He includes venture capitalists and academics such as John Maynard Keynes and Paul Samuelson. And, of course, the founder of passive investing himself – Jack Bogle. It is a varied but comprehensive list, and rather than simply describe who they are and what they did, Matthew looks closely at their relative performance and impact and – crucially – digs down into what investors today could feasibly adopt from each of them.

He also rates them. To answer critics who might argue that over such a long period one is not comparing like with like, Matthew has avoided using over-elaborate assessment criteria and opted for a simple (and not too serious) hotel-style star-rating system of up to five stars in four categories. To avoid spoiling your enjoyment of the book I will not reveal who wins. I can say that no one gets the maximum score of 20 and that the winner is not the most obvious candidate.

So what can this comparative analysis of elite individual investment performance tell you about the path to successful investment, whether you are a professional fund manager or a private investor?

Most investors and analysts would probably agree with Matthew's main conclusions:

- despite a high level of liquidity, computerisation and the speed of the internet, financial markets are still not perfect and there are profitable anomalies to be discovered

- there are many different routes to investment success – and no one silver bullet

- it is important to be open-minded and flexible in one's approach, but patience usually has its own rewards and too much chopping and changing can have negative results

- the stock market is a zero-sum game – for every buyer there has to be seller and both believe they are being astute; if you feel you have an edge you should therefore back it to the hilt

- many traders live by the motto 'sell your losers and let your winners run' but sometimes it pays to buy (or hold) when a price is falling and be ready to buy more later, but whatever the tactic it *always* pays to have an exit plan.

Based on my own long view of 40 years, I would also offer the following observations, a number of which chime with Matthew's findings on these 20 all-time top investors:

1. Timing can be everything. This applies to all forms of investment – not just selling before a fall or trying to work out when a price has bottomed. In venture capital some of the best business plans have missed out on funding because sentiment turned in a matter of days, prompted by some media scare. As Warren Buffett said: "the stock market is a device for transferring money from the impatient to the patient".

2. You can never know too much. Some institutional investors and their advisors get so keen to do a deal that they ignore the need for comprehensive marketing and management due diligence or overlook any negative findings that emerge from such analysis. In the words of Benjamin Graham, "investment is most successful when it is businesslike".

3. Learn to spot brand value. A lot of companies claim to own a brand when in fact what they have is merely some degree of market awareness. Real brands have customers who buy their products or services *when others*

are cheaper or more readily available. Brands generally experience faster than average share price growth with high market rankings (e.g. Apple), leading to significant gains in market share. Experience has shown that brands take years to build but can be destroyed quickly. As Peter Lynch said: "stocks are not lottery tickets".

4. Beware of straight-line forecasting – during the dotcom boom a senior institutional investor said to me that he was sick and tired of reading prospectuses where revenue and profit forecasts were simply extrapolated forward with no kink in the curve. No matter how well-managed, every business has its ups and downs. Again, in the words of Peter Lynch, "You get recessions and stock market declines. If you don't understand that's going to happen, then you're not ready – you won't do well in the markets."

5. Be suspicious of personality cults. We live in a world of celebrities, not just in entertainment but in business. People are often blinded by the past reputations of company chairpersons and CEOs and will back them to repeat the successes of the past even when analysis suggests it is improbable – or impossible – for them to do so. Vision and good management are a necessary but not sufficient condition for success. But as Benjamin Graham points out, "Even the intelligent investor is likely to need considerable willpower to keep from following the crowd".

6. Beware of market sentiment. When I was broadcasting the *Financial Report* on BBC Radio 4 back in the 1970s we used to refer vaguely to movements in market sentiment when we were not too sure why an index or particular shares had moved up or down. Following the crowd can sometimes be successful but it is often what is not fashionable that produces the best returns over time. Benjamin Graham said: "Investors should purchase stocks like they purchase groceries, not like they purchase perfume."

7. Boring companies can make you money. When I worked at the *Investors Chronicle* the companies editor would regularly apply a 'buy' recommendation to companies that no one had ever heard of but which were well run and had cash and (despite that) were trading well below net asset value. It pays to look for the anomalies in the market. In the words of Christopher Browne, "Value stocks are about as exciting as watching grass grow, but have you ever noticed just how much your grass grows in a week?"

It is often said that the modern world of investing is dominated by big, well-resourced funds. Given the size and speed of global financial transactions across integrated markets, the scope for the individual private investor to be active in the market directly rather than simply a passive investor in tracker funds is limited. However, while passive investing is certainly (as Matthew points out) a perfectly legitimate – indeed for some the best – choice, he is an optimist when it comes to the ability of the individual to succeed as an investor.

After reading *Superinvestors*, I think you will be too.

Clive Moffatt

June 2017

Clive Moffatt has over 40 years of experience as an international business and management consultant. A graduate of LSE (1971), he is a former Treasury economist, merchant banker (Guinness Peat Group), financial editor at the BBC and business editor of Investors Chronicle. *His consultancy, Moffatt Associates, was established in 1988.*

INTRODUCTION

Opportunities for Ordinary Investors

A world of highly paid
coin-flippers?

EVER SINCE THE global financial crisis, professional money managers have come under the spotlight like never before. The main complaint is that they charge too much yet deliver surprisingly little. The most pessimistic studies suggest that only a handful of active managers manage to beat their respective indices over an extended period. While other studies paint a more sympathetic picture, the overall message seems to be that it's difficult to beat the market over the long run and that most investment professionals are nothing more than highly paid coin-flippers.

Indeed, the picture seems so bleak that an increasing number of experts think that opting for passive investing, where you put money into low-cost funds that aim to track the stock market, is a no-brainer. This message seems to be getting through to the public, and they have been pulling their money out of active management and putting it into passive funds instead. With many large institutions and pension funds following suit, and regulators making life harder for the remaining managed funds, there is increasing speculation that active investment may be on its way to extinction, aside from a few niche areas.

There's nothing wrong with passive investing. Indeed, if you don't have the time to pick shares, and little interest in learning about the stock market, it is probably the best option. Jack Bogle, who launched the world's first index fund, is rightly regarded as one of the greatest investors in history, and earns a chapter in this book. However, even if the majority of professionals fail to beat their benchmarks, a significant number have added value for their investors, even after taking fees into account. What's more, a small minority have beaten the market over an extended period by a substantial margin. This proves that it is indeed possible to get more than just the average return.

At the same time the barriers to entry for ordinary investors have tumbled. In the past, the opportunities for investing money were limited, transaction costs were high and the playing field was heavily tilted towards the professionals. Thanks to a combination of online brokerages, changes to the rules and the rise of spread betting, the individual can go head-to-head with the professionals. The rise of equity crowdfunding and peer-to-peer products means that even areas such as venture capital are more accessible than they have ever been, while the rise of the internet has shrunk the world when it comes to investing.

This means investors don't have to sit back and accept a choice between mediocre fund managers and an index fund, but can take matters into their own hands and invest their money themselves. Of course, it isn't easy to do this successfully, so investors need to come up with viable strategies. Such strategies must fulfil two criteria: they must give them a good chance of success, and they must be realistic in terms of the time, energy and temperament they require of an investor. The best way to come up with a plan, and to make up for the fact that professional investors have more experience, is to look at the select few who have been extremely successful.

Greatest investors

In 2016 I began a weekly column for *MoneyWeek* magazine (where I work) profiling some of these great investors, looking at their strategies, performance, best investments and the lessons that ordinary investors could learn from them. After the first few columns I realised that many of the individual careers were so interesting and informative that they deserved a more detailed investigation. I also discovered that books covering this area, though useful, tended to stick to one style of investing, and usually focused on contemporary investors at the expense of those who had made their money in earlier times.

I therefore decided to select 20 particularly successful investors worthy of further attention and to explore their investing careers in more depth. These investors have been selected because of their performance, longevity, influence and the extent to which retail investors can emulate them. They include both American and British investors, and cover a wide range of historical periods, beginning with David Ricardo at the end of the 18th century and Jesse Livermore in the early 20th century, through to those who are still running money today.

I've included examples of short-term traders (Ricardo, Livermore, Soros and Steinhardt), value investors (Graham, Buffett, Bolton and Woodford) and growth investors (Fisher, Rowe Price, Lynch and Train). I have also included some venture capitalists (Doriot and Kleiner/Perkins). While most retail investors won't be able to put money directly into private companies – though even this is changing with crowdfunding – the careers of these venture capitalists provide some useful insights into technology investing.

The final six chapters are focused on those investors who don't really fit into any of the previous four categories, but still deserve a place in the investment pantheon. John Templeton played a key role in convincing the American public that it should look beyond the American stock market. Robert Wilson used the power of compound interest and some shrewd investments to build a fortune that nearly reached a billion dollars, and showed how short-selling can be used consistently to boost returns, as well as just reducing risk. Edward Thorp was the first 'quant', using computer power and statistics to spot (and ultimately exploit) investment opportunities.

John Maynard Keynes switched between various strategies. After trying (and failing) to use his knowledge of macroeconomics to make money in the currency market, he eventually found success as a value investor. As previously mentioned, Jack Bogle pioneered index investing, overcoming considerable ridicule to turn it into a major investment strategy. Paul Samuelson is primarily remembered as the economist who developed the efficient market theory, which states that markets can't be beaten. However, he played a key role in an important hedge fund and was also a successful private investor.

Rating the investors

While the primary aim of this book is to educate (and entertain) readers by talking about some amazing investors, this book will also attempt to rate them, to see which ones were the most important. In line with the criteria used for inclusion, they will be rated on four metrics: their overall performance, their longevity, their influence on other investors and investing in general, and how easy it is for ordinary investors to emulate them. To enable direct comparisons to be made between investors who had different styles and operated in different periods, each of them are awarded hotel-style stars. These range from one star, where an investor made very little impact in an area, to five, where they have made an exceptional contribution.

In the case of performance, the big focus is on how they did relative to the stock market (usually the S&P 500 or the FTSE 100), after their fees are taken into account. In cases where data on returns isn't available, for example with Ricardo, their success is judged by how much money they made. Consistency is important, so those who managed funds that ended up failing, or who went bankrupt several times, get a lower ranking even if they ended up making money. Given that the most basic goal of an investor is to make money, nearly all the investors have four or five-star ratings in this area (apart from Bogle, who only gets three stars).

Longevity and performance are strongly interlinked, because achieving sustained performance over a long career is much harder than doing it for a couple of years. Those whose careers lasted several decades get the full five stars, while those whose careers lasted just over a decade don't do as well. In this case the primary focus is on how long they directly managed money or invested, rather than any time they spent in more general financial roles. As with performance, most of the investors get high marks in this category, though there are a few who get relatively low scores.

Another criteria that is frequently overlooked when evaluating investors is the ease with which non-professionals can implement their strategies. The obvious example of this is Warren Buffett. He has been tremendously successful in making money over a career spanning six decades. However, most of Berkshire Hathaway's investments are in privately listed companies, which members of the public cannot directly own. Similarly, short-term trading requires a lot of spare time and emotional investment, as many of those who gave up their jobs to trade shares during the internet bubble in the late 1990s found out the hard way.

As well as making money, investors can contribute to investing by influencing the way people invest. In some cases this can involve developing a new approach to investing, like Philip Fisher's focus on finding companies that can grow their earnings rapidly over a long period. Or an investor can leave a mark by launching new financial products, like Jack Bogle and his development of index funds. However, it's important to note that, by itself, name recognition or celebrity doesn't necessarily guarantee a high rating in this area. For example, George Soros is a well-known philanthropist and played a big role in Britain leaving the ERM, which in turn had a significant impact on British politics. However, his financial theories, such as 'reflexivity', have left little mark.

CHAPTER I
Jesse Livermore

═══

The Trend-Following
Boy Plunger

A self-made man

A SK ANY EXPERIENCED trader to recommend a book and they will probably at least mention *Reminiscences of a Stock Operator* by Edwin Lefèvre, the fictionalised memoirs of speculator Jesse Livermore. The fact that a book first published in 1923 is widely considered recommended reading nearly a century later should tell you something about the respect in which Livermore was held among stock traders. As well as being instructive, the multiple rise, fall and comebacks of the 'boy plunger' is also a fascinating story in itself.

Another striking thing about Livermore's career is how he funded it. While all successful traders and investors like to think of themselves as self-made, for most this is only partly correct. They might have come up with their ideas themselves but typically they will have done their trading and investing for an investment trust, hedge fund or bank, and then collected a share of the profits or a management fee. However, instead of using other people's money, Livermore's investments involved his own cash. The reversals that he experienced had a direct impact on his standard of living.

From the farm to Wall Street
via bucket shops

Livermore was born in 1877 on a farm near Shrewsbury, Massachusetts, in the northeastern United States. Despite showing promise at school, especially at maths, his father forced him to leave at the age of 14 in the expectation that Jesse would help run the family farm. Defying his father's wishes, and with the approval of his mother, Livermore ran away to nearby Boston with only $5 in his pocket (equivalent to $134 in today's money). He quickly got a job at the brokerage Paine Webber, updating the price board so that brokers and customers could see how much individual stocks cost.

While this menial job would only pay him $6 a week, seeing how the price of stocks moved up, down and sideways, would give him a knack for predicting when they were about to rise and fall. Within a year he was buying and selling shares in the bucket shops. These were gambling parlours where you could cheaply buy stocks on credit. Instead of a normal brokerage, no actual shares were bought and sold – instead you would get paid on the difference between the price that you bought them and the price on the ticker.

This primitive form of spread betting relied on the fact that most punters would cancel each other out, enabling the bucket shop to pocket its commission. In the case of thinly traded stocks, the house hoped that the punters would eventually lose their money, as due to the amount of leverage employed even a 10% move against a bettor would wipe his stake out. However, Livermore was able to consistently beat the market, using leverage to make huge profits. Eventually the bucket shops tired of him making money and he was banned from all of them in Boston, but not before he had accumulated $10,000.

This enabled him to start trading through proper brokers. However, he initially found things difficult because brokers, who themselves had to trade through traders on the floor of the stock exchange, took time to execute his trades and weren't always able to get the best prices. As a result, he briefly returned to the bucket shops (supported by a loan from his then broker, EF

Hutton) in order to rebuild his stake after an early loss. However, from 1897 to his second (and final) bankruptcy in 1934, Livermore played both the commodity and the stock markets.

Reading the tape like a conductor

His main strategy was 'tape reading', or trend following as it is more popularly known. This involved monitoring the price movements of stocks (literally reading the stock ticker tape on which they were printed), looking to see if there was a sudden change in direction. If this change continued with enough force he would then follow it. At first he would stake a relatively small amount. However, if the trend continued he would gradually increase his position until it became much bigger. He would only close his position when he was convinced that the trend had ended.

This strategy meant that he didn't attempt to buy stocks at the absolute bottom or short them at their absolute peak. Instead, he felt that traders should be happy to wait until they had already advanced before piling in, and was particularly interested in shares that were making new highs. As he put it, "Do you wish to gamble blindly in the hope of getting a great big profit or do you wish to speculate intelligently and get a smaller but much more probable profit?"

Unlike other traders who felt that you should ignore all fundamental factors, such as the balance between supply and demand, Livermore frequently used these factors to guide his overall view, especially when trading commodities. However, he thought that if you just relied on fundamental factors to determine whether a stock or commodity was properly priced you ran the risk of being right too early, and therefore losing out while you waited for the market to catch up. He also believed that the market is reasonably good at anticipating future earnings and dividends, so these factors are already priced in.

If Livermore had mixed views about the value of fundamental analysis, he was scathing about the value of tips from outsiders. Although insider trading had been illegal in the US since 1909, it was common for insiders to drop hints about how a company was doing. It was also relatively common for speculators to group together in an attempt to corner commodity markets. His view was that most of those giving advice didn't have a real knowledge (or understanding) of what was happening. Even in the few cases where they had genuine knowledge, it was more likely than not that they were giving out false advice in order to further their own agendas.

For instance, Livermore gave the example of a company director who boasted about how well his firm was doing. While the stock initially surged, it quickly fell back. Livermore later found out that the director knew the company was really doing badly and was quietly selling his holdings. Livermore admits that he didn't always follow his rule of ignoring tips and outside advice, especially in his early career, occasionally succumbing to temptation. However, he would claim in *Reminiscences* that a reversal early on in his career, when a friend convinced him to abandon a long position in a company just before the stock soared, finally convinced him to ignore advice from outsiders. He would advise investors to write down in a notebook '*Beware of Inside Information...All Inside Information*'.

From rags to riches to rags

Livermore's wealth fluctuated dramatically over his career. By 1901 he had repaid Hutton's loan and had built his trading capital up to $50,000 ($1.4m). Then disaster struck: a reversal that year cleared him out, destroying his first marriage (after his wife refused to pawn her jewellery) and forcing him to return to the bucket shops.

A few years later, after greatly profiting from the stock market panic of 1907, he had built up $3m worth of cash ($78m). However, a series of bad trades, most notably in cotton, first reduced his capital by 90% and then eventually forced him to declare bankruptcy in 1912.

Of course, Livermore couldn't be kept down and by 1917 he was rich enough to not only repay all his creditors in full, but also set up a $500,000 ($9.23m) trust fund. By the 1920s he would be rich enough to own multiple properties and a 300-foot yacht. After the Wall Street Crash his wealth was estimated at $100m ($1.4bn). However, by 1934 he would be bankrupt again. This time there would be no comeback. Due to this failure, and various personal problems, such as the near death of his son, Jesse Jr, he would commit suicide in 1940. However, he was still able to repay his creditors and he left an estate of $5m in cash, jewellery and other assets.

The man who brought down the market

The trade that cemented Livermore's reputation, and also earned him a degree of notoriety, was his decision to short the stock market before the Wall Street Crash in October 1929. While a handful of other investors were astute (or lucky) enough to do the same, they did so as the result of instinct, with Joseph Kennedy famously selling all his shares after his shoeshine boy started giving him stock tips. In contrast, Livermore's decision was prompted by several factors and timed to perfection.

First, as the stock market boom reached its peak in the late 1920s, he observed that even relatively ordinary stocks were trading at high multiples of their profits over the last 12 months, a sign that investors were becoming wildly optimistic about the future. Livermore also became aware that large numbers of ordinary people were playing the stock market using borrowed money, buying stocks with only a partial down payment, sometimes as little as 10%. While he and other professionals regularly employed leverage themselves, he realised that this left average investors badly exposed in the event of a crash. It also meant that the stock market boom depended on investors borrowing ever increasing amounts of money. Since this was unsustainable, Livermore realised that this had to come to an end – and soon.

At the same time, Livermore noticed that the stocks that had risen most strongly at the start of the boom were now either peaking or even falling. He believed that this was a sign that the bull market was running out of steam. With both technical and fundamental signs pointing to a reversal, he turned his attention to how to take advantage of this. As long as the overall market was still rising, he knew that if he simply shorted stocks he could be left badly exposed. So he first focused on selling all the shares that he owned, which he did by the summer of 1929.

Livermore could now begin to turn his full attention to shorting the market. He began to send probes, by shorting small amounts of key shares, just to see how the market would react. Initially, these probes failed, as the market kept rising, costing him $250,000 – a huge amount of money but only a tiny part of his fortune. He then took a second series of short positions. When these positions started succeeding, Livermore realised that the game was up. He started aggressively shorting stocks, just in time for Black Thursday on 24 October 1929, when the market plunged 11% in one day.

By December, the market had more than halved from its peak in September. Livermore made millions from his short positions, leading to his net worth being estimated at over $100m. Indeed, his success was so great that he was accused of being a key part of a large conspiracy designed to bring down the market. He was forced to issue a statement saying that he hadn't been working with anyone else and that the market had collapsed because it was overvalued. Despite this denial, he was forced to hire a private detective as a bodyguard a few months later.

Blowing money on other investments

While Livermore was a skilled trader, he was not as good at other types of investing. Indeed, he admitted that his forays into investments outside of the stock market – usually at the behest of his friends – were nothing short of disastrous. His involvement with the Mizner Development Corporation in 1925, a syndicate aiming to create a resort in Florida, led to him being personally sued by disgruntled investors. This was despite the fact that he and other prominent directors had complained to the promoter that it was implying that they were underwriting the project, when in fact they were not.

As Livermore would put it in *How to Trade in Stocks*, "I have never been able to make a dollar outside of Wall Street. But I have lost many millions of dollars, which I had taken from Wall Street, 'investing' in other ventures". He mentions "real estate in the Florida boom, oil wells, airplane manufacturing, and the perfecting and marketing of products based on new inventions." Livermore once admitted that he was so bad at outside projects that a friend whom he had approached for additional investment bluntly told him: "Livermore, you will never make a success in any business outside your own."

What Livermore's story teaches us

Strictly speaking, Livermore was a trader, making money from short-term movements in prices, not a long-term investor. While this approach can be extremely lucrative in terms of returns, it can be extremely volatile. The fact that even a legend like Livermore experienced wild swings in fortune shows that this approach is not for the fainthearted. It was also labour-intensive, since it required him to spend a lot of time monitoring market prices and researching potential trades. Those who have work and family commitments may therefore struggle to replicate his success.

Perhaps the closest modern parallel is with spread betting, where you bet on movements in the prices of shares and commodities. While some ordinary investors have made a huge amount of money from spread betting it can also be very expensive if you don't know what you're doing. If you go down that path, you must limit your trading to money that you can afford to lose.

One of the keys to Livermore's success was his tight money management. Unlike an investor, a trader can't afford to take a long-term perspective. Livermore believed in quickly closing trades that were losing money, and freely admitted that he would have found the sustained losses taken by long-term investors intolerable. Most spread-betting firms allow you to set stop-losses that will automatically trigger if a position goes against you by a certain amount. Conversely, he believed in letting winning positions run until the price data suggested that the trend was about to end. He believed in putting a percentage of profits from any winning trade aside into a separate account (which allowed him to retain a substantial fortune after his bankruptcies).

Finally, Livermore's sad end should be a reminder about the need to retain a degree of perspective. Although trading can be a way to enhance your wealth, it should not become an obsession. Indeed, before you start trading or investing you need to ask yourself whether you are happy with the possibility that you may lose your entire stake. If not, you should choose a less stressful investment philosophy.

As the saying goes, if your investments are keeping you awake, you need to sell to your sleeping point.

RATING
JESSE LIVERMORE

Performance: *Building an entire fortune from scratch is clearly an achievement. However, Livermore's multiple bankruptcies, including the one that ultimately led in part to his final depression clearly detracts from his performance, even if he was still able to pass on substantial funds to his wife and children.* (★★★★)

Longevity: *Livermore's career as a trader lasted over four decades from 1891 to his final bankruptcy in 1934.* (★★★★★)

Influence: Reminiscences of a Stock Operator, *a fictionalised version of his memoirs, is regarded as one of the most influential books on trading ever written.* (★★★★★)

Ease of replication: *Day trading is an incredibly stressful and time-consuming way to make money, with a high probability of failure. However, even those taking longer-term positions can learn a lot from Livermore.* (★★)

Overall rating: 16 out of 20

CHAPTER 2
David Ricardo

═══

The Napoleonic Speculator

Introduction

I F YOU'VE EVER studied economics, you'll have come across David Ricardo. One of the earliest economic theorists, many of the ideas that he came up with are still studied today. Indeed, his theory of 'comparative advantage' (the idea that countries can maximise production by specialising in what they are best at producing) remains the cornerstone of modern trade policy. He was also an influential political figure in early 19th century Britain, arguing for the repeal of the Corn Laws and for changes in the way that the government borrowed money and managed the national debt.

However, most people don't know that he was also an extremely well-respected financier and trader. Indeed, Ricardo's fame was such that an obituary in *The Times* (written after his death) speculated that in the future he'd be remembered primarily for his ability to make money on the stock market rather than as a thinker. Obviously the reverse turned out to be the case, and he made his money in an era when the financial markets were still in their infancy (the first members-only stock exchange was created in 1801 and the first rulebook was introduced in 1812). However, his life story still contains important lessons for modern investors.

How did he start out?

Ricardo was born in London in 1772 and left education at age 14 to work for his father, a successful stockbroker. However, seven years later he eloped with the daughter of a Quaker and became a Unitarian. This permanently estranged him from his parents, and forced him to make a living as a stock jobber – a role where you functioned as both a market maker and floor trader (the division between floor traders and brokers lasted in the UK until Big Bang in 1986). While jobbers were allowed to buy and sell a wide range of stocks and bonds, Ricardo primarily traded government debt (known as 'consols').

Although he was primarily known for his jobbing activities, Ricardo was also respected enough to become a loan contractor, leading various syndicates that bid for government debt. The idea was that these syndicates, which would be made up of wealthy private investors, would compete with existing banks to lend money to the government, thus enabling the government to borrow money more cheaply at a time when finances were strained by the Napoleonic Wars, which began in 1803 and caused the national debt to increase dramatically.

Ricardo's syndicate would fail in its first attempt to be included in the government loan. However, the next year it was more successful, becoming the first to break the monopoly of private banks, as it was allowed to subscribe to a £14.2m portion (around £1.01bn in today's money). Overall, between 1811 and 1815, Ricardo's syndicates were involved in loans worth £158m (£10.5bn), though these were shared with banks and other syndicates (and of course Ricardo's syndicate had many individual members). Ricardo retired from finance shortly after the Battle of Waterloo in 1815, though he continued to manage his own investments, making loans to nearby industrialists. By the time of his death he was speculating on whether French bonds would hold their value during the Franco-Spanish war.

Taking advantage of hysteria

For most of his career, Ricardo employed two main strategies. Firstly, he engaged in what people would today describe as 'pairs trading'. He would look for bonds that, while not identical, generally behaved in a similar way. Whenever the price of them diverged, he would buy the one that was relatively cheaper and short the one that had become more expensive. The idea was that, if he was correct in his judgement of the proper relationship between the two (which he usually was), the prices on the two instruments would eventually start to converge. This meant that any losses on one position would be outweighed by his profits on the other.

Ricardo also supplemented this approach with the occasional speculative position. Ricardo was a natural contrarian who believed that the market tended to overreact to short-term events. However, he felt the best way to take advantage of this was to adopt a momentum-based approach that aimed to get ahead of the market. As a result, he looked out for news that would push stocks higher so that he could buy in anticipation of further price gains. Similarly, if he felt that negative news would discourage investors, he would sell. Ricardo was one of the first to believe in keeping risk low by closing losing positions while letting winners run.

Small profits add up to a lavish lifestyle

Although Ricardo never revealed the exact amount of money that he made, the evidence suggests that his trading activities brought in a stream of profits. While the sums were relatively small (usually a few hundred pounds at most) their consistency and frequency allowed him to accumulate a large amount of trading capital. At the time he left his father in 1793 he had only £800, with the remainder of his capital funded by a loan from sympathetic bankers. However, by 1801 he was successful enough to have traded over £1m worth of consols in a single year (equivalent to £69m at 2015 prices).

This success allowed him to fund an increasingly lavish lifestyle. When he married in 1793 he lived in a small house in Kennington, then a semi-rural London suburb, at an annual rent of £18 (£1,904). By 1812 he was paying £450 (£27,000) a year for a large mansion in fashionable Grosvenor Square (the site of the US Embassy). In 1814 he would buy Gatcombe Park, a country estate in Gloucestershire, for £60,000 (£3.79m). Ricardo and his family used Gatcombe to throw frequent elaborate parties.

After he retired from finance, Ricardo was able to buy a seat in Parliament in return for a loan of £25,000 (£1.7m), enabling him to take his seat in early 1819. By the time of his death in 1823, his estate was estimated to be worth over £700,000 (£57.2m). However, since this didn't take into account the appreciation in the value of his property, the true value was probably higher.

Ricardo's Waterloo

Nothing defined Ricardo's status as a legendary speculator more than his behaviour immediately before and after the Battle of Waterloo in June 1815. While there are several versions of what happened, the most well known comes from the economist Paul Samuelson, who wrote extensively about Ricardo's economic theories (and is featured later in this book). In a journal article written shortly before his death, Samuelson claimed that Ricardo had hired an assistant to observe the battle and quickly bring the news back to him. As a result, he knew about the outcome of the battle before anyone else.

While most people would have taken advantage of the situation to buy more bonds, Samuelson claimed that Ricardo supposedly chose an even more devious strategy. "On his customary chair at the Exchange, he sold British Treasury stuff again and again. The other traders saw this, and suspecting that he would know the true story, they joined in the selling.

Then, suddenly, Ricardo reversed course and bought and bought." The result of these transactions was "his biggest coup ever", which "enabled him to retire from active trading and become a passive rentier-investor for the rest of his life".

Those who enjoy tales of financial cunning will relish the cold-bloodedness of this gigantic bluff (though such behaviour would now be viewed as illegal market manipulation). However, historians have been unable to find direct evidence either of him having advance knowledge of the outcome before anyone else or of him spreading rumours of Britain's defeat. Ricardo would also downplay the amount of money that he had made. Indeed, in a letter to John Stuart Mill (another famous economic and political thinker) he stated that, while he was now rich, "I am not 'Bless me how rich!!'".

Still, there is no doubt that he did make a lot of money during the period. Napoleon's escape from Elba and triumphant return in March 2015, three months before the Battle of Waterloo, led to widespread fears of another prolonged conflict, or even an invasion of Britain. This pushed the prices of consols down to a low level (possibly helped by some judicious selling on the part of Ricardo immediately before the auction). Ricardo not only got his syndicate to successfully bid for £36m worth of government debt, but personally invested a large amount of his wealth in the deal. While his friend Malthus, who had also subscribed, insisted on cashing in immediately for a small profit, Ricardo held on to most of his share.

Indeed, Ricardo seems to have taken advantage of a temporary dip in price, after counter-rumours of a British defeat began to circulate in the days after the initial reports, to load up further. As a result, a fortnight after the battle had ended Ricardo said that he had plunged his entire wealth into gilts, and had already "been a considerable gainer by the loan". Months later Ricardo would confirm that he was now "sufficiently rich to satisfy all my desires, and the reasonable desires of all those about me". Overall, Ricardo's obituary in *The Sunday Times* would claim that he had made £1m from speculation in government bonds during this time (equivalent to £66.2m in today's money).

Difference between investing and speculation

On the face of it, Ricardo's behavior seems contradictory. Excluding his pairs trading, he spent most of his life betting with the crowd. However, his most famous (and profitable) investment involved doing the exact opposite of what everyone else was doing (i.e. lending money to the government and buying bonds when everyone else was panicking about a French invasion). However, this isn't as illogical as it seems. Indeed, it illustrates how the time frame of an investment should determine your strategy – or, in other words, that short-term trading differs from long-term investing.

Indeed, Ricardo seems to have anticipated the large amount of academic literature showing that in the short run stocks exhibit positive momentum. In other words, those that go up in price are more likely to keep rising, while those that do badly will continue to underperform. For example, a 1993 study by Narasimhan Jegadeesh and Sheridan Titman found that if you had bought the best-performing stocks over brief holding periods and then held them for an equal length of time, you would have outperformed the market. This effect isn't just limited to the stock market, with Lukas Menkhoff of Cass Business School finding that going with the best-performing currencies generated outsize returns.

However, over the longer run, this momentum effect starts to diminish, and eventually reverses. Indeed, a 1985 study by Werner De Bondt and Richard Thaler found that portfolios of the worst-performing stocks over extended periods, such as several years, tended to outperform those that had done the best. Indeed, some of the most brutal bear markets in history have been followed by equally strong rallies. For example, after the stock market more than halved in the 18 months from September 2007, it then nearly doubled in just under two years. It therefore makes a lot of sense to do what Ricardo did, and be a crowd-follower for short-term trades, but a contrarian with longer-run positions.

As David Ricardo's contemporary Baron Rothschild said, "the time to buy is when there's blood in the streets".

RATING
DAVID RICARDO

Performance: *After being disowned by his father, David Ricardo managed to use his trading abilities to eventually create a substantial fortune by the standards of the day. Still, even adjusted for inflation, his final net worth is relatively small by the standards of modern hedge-fund titans. (★★★★)*

Longevity: *Ricardo began his career in 1793 and retired after the Battle of Waterloo in 1815. However, he was a major player for around 14 years. (★★★★)*

Influence: *While his economic writings are still studied today, his influence on investing was much more modest. (★★)*

Ease of replication: *As with Livermore, it is relatively hard for ordinary investors to carry out the large number of short-term trades that Ricardo used to create his fortune. (★★)*

Overall rating: 12 out of 20

CHAPTER 3
George Soros

The Alchemist Who Broke
the Bank of England

Feared rather than loved

ALONG WITH WARREN Buffett, George Soros is the only living investor whose name the average person on the street might recognise. However, while Warren Buffett has attained 'national treasure' status, George Soros is feared as well as respected. On the one hand his comments on economics regularly make the headlines. His philanthropy, especially towards pro-democracy organisations, has also won him respect around the world. Indeed, his efforts in helping Eastern Europe develop a civil society after the collapse of the Iron Curtain were so influential that they have been dubbed a "second Marshall Plan".

However, this increased visibility has made him a convenient scapegoat for when things go wrong. The most notorious example of this came in 1997 when the then-prime minister of Malaysia, Mahathir bin Mohamad, blamed him for causing the Asian financial crisis. Of course, the crisis was clearly caused by poor economic policies, not the actions of some shadowy cabal, and Mohamad was later forced to admit these conspiratorial claims were nonsense. However, the very fact that some people believe that Soros is in a position to determine the fate of countries is a testament to his financial acumen, status within the financial community, and long track record of success.

From immigrant to billionaire

Soros was born in Budapest, Hungary in 1930. After surviving the Nazi occupation of Hungary, Soros would eventually study philosophy at the London School of Economics, doing a bachelor's degree, followed by a master's in philosophy, supporting himself with a combination of menial jobs, including being a railway porter and a waiter, and a small grant from a charity. While he initially had dreams of becoming an academic, he realised that he was not good enough, so he turned his attention towards the idea of becoming an investment banker. After several false starts, he was hired as a trainee at the merchant bank Singer & Friedlander in 1954.

Although he was quickly promoted to the position of arbitrage trader, he believed that his prospects of further advancement were limited, as the firm was reluctant to give much responsibility to junior staff members. As a result, he moved to America, taking advantage of his knowledge of European markets to get a similar job with the New York firm F. M. Mayer. He would later move to Wertheim & Co. Soros would make one last stab at trying to become an academic philosopher, revising his master's thesis between 1961–3. However, after it got only a lukewarm reaction from the LSE professor Karl Popper, Soros abandoned his dreams of academia and completely focused on making money.

Soros's big breakthrough came after he joined Arnhold and S. Bleichroeder in 1963. Starting out as an analyst, he would became director of research four years later. In 1966 the firm agreed to set up a model fund with $100,000 ($729,000 at 2015 prices). As a result of this Bleichroeder let Soros set up two real funds: First Eagle in 1967 and Double Eagle in 1969. However, legal changes that made it difficult for Soros to receive a share of the profits while still at Bleichroeder, and a desire for independence, meant that Soros decided to strike out on his own.

By 1973 Soros formally cut ties with the parent company by resigning from the First Eagle fund and giving the investors the choice of either going with the Soros fund (now known as the Quantum Fund) or sticking with Bleichroeder. Until 1988, Soros would retain sole control over Quantum. However, from the late 1980s onwards, the sheer size of the fund, as well as Soros's interest in philanthropy, meant that he would delegate increasing parts of the day-to-day management to a small team of elite fund managers, most notably Stanley Druckenmiller (Druckenmiller would work with Quantum from 1988 to 2000).

However, this didn't mean that Soros gave up managing money. Not only did he retain overall control, but he would frequently step in to take large positions himself. In 2011, he would close the fund to outside investors and return the money that they had invested. As a result, it now just runs Soros's own money.

Using reflexivity

Soros is a 'global macro' investor. This means that instead of restricting himself to one asset class, such as shares, he has focused on a wide range of currencies, bonds and commodities. In particular, he has made a lot of highly leveraged bets on currency movements and government bonds based on his macroeconomic predictions. He has frequently used borrowed money in his currency and bond bets, hoping that this will boost his returns. While the vast majority of his investments are in liquid assets that he can buy and sell quickly, he has also taken stakes in privately listed companies and invested in property.

Soros's approach is generally that of a value investor, buying assets cheap in the hope that they will rise in value. However, he has developed his own theory of financial markets, called 'reflexivity', which he attempted to outline in his 1987 book *The Alchemy of Finance*. Basically, this boils down to two ideas: firstly, that markets are driven more by participants' behaviour than reason, leading to assets being mispriced. Secondly – and unlike traditional value investing, which focuses on the idea that market prices will eventually revert to the fundamentals – Soros believes this behaviour can end up *changing* the fundamentals. As a result, he believes that in some cases bubbles can end up persisting.

Soros has been involved with multiple funds, several of which have merged and de-merged, making it hard to measure his performance exactly. Some would argue that Druckenmiller, and other managers Soros delegated responsibility to, deserve part of the credit for Quantum's excellent performance. However, there is no doubt that Soros himself has been extraordinarily successful. It has been estimated by the *New York Times* that between 1969 and 2011 the Quantum Fund produced an average return of around 20%, compared with less than 10% for the stock market during that period. Despite a large amount of philanthropy, Soros's net worth has been estimated by Bloomberg at around $24.4bn (as of 2017).

Breaking the Bank of England

George Soros's most famous trade was his successful bet against sterling in 1992, which earned him the nickname of "the man who broke the Bank of England". In 1979 eight European countries agreed to form the European Rates Mechanism (ERM). The idea was to tie their currencies together, severely limiting the amount that they could fluctuate against each other. The hope was that this would boost trade by reducing exchange-rate volatility. By stopping countries devaluing their way out of an economic crisis, it would also force them to be fiscally disciplined and pass pro-growth reforms.

In 1990, after much internal debate, the UK finally joined the ERM. The problem was that it joined at a very high exchange rate. This would make British exports much less competitive, hitting economic growth. At the same time the German central bank, the de facto leader of the ERM, was concerned about the inflationary impact of reunification and decided to hike interest rates. This meant that the British government had two choices: stay in the ERM at the cost of strangling the economy, or devalue to stimulate the economy, a policy that was incompatible with ERM membership.

Since Soros believed that the British housing market and economy were both unable to withstand further rises, he concluded that Britain would have to leave the ERM. Furthermore, he believed that once the financial markets lost confidence in Britain's commitment to the ERM, they would start dumping pounds. This would raise the costs of keeping the pound at the required level to above those that were politically acceptable. In short, even if the British government wanted to stay in the ERM, the perception that Britain was going to leave would force it out — a clear example of expectations shifting the fundamentals, as predicted by Soros's own theory of reflexivity.

Starting in the summer of 1992, Soros therefore decided to take a large short position against sterling, borrowing £5bn and using the money to buy Deutsche Marks. Overall, his bets against the pound falling against the D-Mark would end up totalling $10bn.

On 15 September 1992, traders began dumping the pound in the anticipation of an imminent devaluation. Initially, the Bank of England attempted to defend sterling by buying up pounds, with chief dealer Jim Trott later saying that in the space of four hours it had bought more than it ever bought before or since. The following day it would hike rates to 12%, and then 15%. However, this failed to stop the selling, so the government threw in the towel, announcing that Britain was leaving the ERM (Italy would also quit). Interest rates were also quickly cut back to 10% (they would fall to under 6% by the start of 1993).

As a result, the pound quickly fell against the D-Mark. While other traders made money from this decline, Soros's huge short position meant that he would net around $1bn directly, with related trades (including shorting the Italian lira) boosting his profits to $2bn in the month following what would become known as Black Wednesday. In contrast, the British government would lose £3.3bn. An interview Soros gave to *The Times* in October led to massive press interest, cementing his reputation as a legendary financier.

Mauled by the Russian bear

Of course, Soros has not always got things right. During the 1990s, Soros spent a lot of money trying to rebuild Russian civil society. Indeed, at one point he donated more money than the US gave Russia in international aid. As a result, he initially stayed clear of any investment in the country, direct or otherwise, because he didn't want to be accused of having a conflict of interest. However, his confidence that economic reforms would lead to an eventual post-Soviet boom meant that the temptation to bet on the country became too great to resist.

In 1994 he made a small investment, which he quickly sold for a profit. Three years later he plunged billions of dollars into the country, including over $1bn into Svyazinvest, a Russian phone company that had recently been privatised. He also continued to invest money, additionally lending several hundred billion dollars to the Russian government directly. However, by August of 1998 it became clear that the Russian economy was in serious trouble, with the country unable to pay its debt. In an attempt to galvanise action, Soros wrote a letter to the *Financial Times* suggesting a $15bn international bailout of Russia, along with other measures to stabilise the country.

However, this letter would badly backfire, causing investors to panic even more. A few days later the Russian government announced that it was not only going to devalue the rouble, but it was going to suspend payments on its debts. This financial chaos caused both the currency and the stock market to plummet as investors rushed for the door. Soros, who by this time was the largest private foreign investor in the country, was badly hit. Indeed, he would publicly admit a few weeks later than he had lost $2bn. Evidence of Soros's abilities as an investor comes from the fact that despite this setback Quantum still managed to make money overall that year.

Lessons from George Soros

George Soros believes that you should only invest in areas where you have an edge, or better understanding than the rest of the market. During his early career as an analyst, Soros's edge was his knowledge of European stocks and companies (which most US investors knew little about). Since running Quantum, his focus has mainly been on the currency and fixed income markets. It is significant that his one big failure was where he stepped outside this area to invest directly in a company. It shows that if you can't understand an investment idea, or feel that you don't have any particular advantage, you should choose something else.

Soros's success also comes from his skill at picking the right people with whom to work. During the early days of Quantum he worked with Jim Rogers, another skilled investor. Similarly, his association with Stanley Druckenmiller proved to be extremely profitable for Quantum. Conversely, he was ruthless at getting rid of managers who turned out to be poor investors (such as Jim Marquez). Something investors might take from this is that, while investment trusts and funds generally underperform the market over the long run (especially after fees are taken into account), a savvy investor can still find some funds which beat the market.

Finally, Soros's experience with Russia shows the importance of staying objective. Of course, there's nothing wrong with avoiding certain sectors or countries for ethical reasons. However, investing in a company or country because you personally like the CEO, or agree with what they are doing, is rarely a good idea. It's interesting to note that while Soros supported Britain remaining in the EU, and warned that voting to leave would damage the economy, this didn't stop him making a sizeable amount of money in the aftermath. Indeed, while he lost money from bets on sterling, he more than made this up through buying put options on global markets and financial institutions (since put options are contracts that give you the right, but not the obligation, to sell an asset at a certain price, they soared in value once the results were known).

RATING
GEORGE SOROS

Performance: *George Soros has been an extremely successful hedge fund investor using his skill to accumulate a fortune estimated at over $25bn.* (★ ★ ★ ★ ★)

Longevity: *George Soros has been involved in investing since the 1950s.* (★ ★ ★ ★ ★)

Influence: *George Soros's philanthropy has been credited with speeding up the fall of the Iron Curtain. His trade against sterling in 1992 was also credited with forcing Britain out of the ERM. However, his actual impact on the world of investing has been more limited, though he was one of the early hedge fund managers.* (★ ★ ★)

Ease of replication: *Soros has been an aggressive trader, especially in currency markets which can be dangerous for the novice trader because of the degree of leverage employed. He has also farmed out an increasing amount of his capital to other managers.* (★ ★)

Overall rating: 15 out of 20

CHAPTER 4
Michael Steinhardt

═══

The Contrarian Hedge Funder

Introduction

MANY PEOPLE LIKE to consider themselves as contrarian investors. Indeed, you could argue that by taking an active position, all traders, even trend followers, are implicitly saying that the market has got it wrong. However, if you define contrarian investors as those who actively seek out opportunities to invest in the opposite direction to everyone else, there are indeed few investors who would meet the criteria. Fewer still have the courage and conviction to use contrarian investing as a core strategy, rather than just another investment tool to be wheeled out on occasion and then forgotten about.

Michael Steinhardt is one of the exceptions. One of the first generation of hedge fund pioneers, he took advantage of the freedom that the structure gave him to take a large number of contrarian positions over a long period. Not only did he have several high-profile successes, but he also generated huge returns over an extended period. He is also someone from whom the average investor can learn a lot.

The sociology of the markets

Born in New York in 1940, Michael Steinhardt graduated early from the University of Pennsylvania with a degree in sociology and statistics in 1960, aged 19. Following this, he got a job in the statistical department of the mutual fund Calvin Bullock, an opportunity that he credits with sparking an interest in the stock market. At the same time he started investing in shares himself, financed by a large loan from his father. After army service and a brief stint with the newsletter *Financial World*, Steinhardt got a job as an analyst with the Wall Street brokerage firm Loeb, Rhoades & Co.

At Loeb, Steinhardt would have a huge amount of success recommending the growth stocks and conglomerates that benefited hugely from the bull market of the 1960s, companies such as Gulf and Western. This success prompted him to set up his own investment fund, Steinhardt, Fine, Berkowitz & Co (SFB), which used the then-novel hedge fund structure. Although technically a partnership between him and two other Pennsylvania alumni, Steinhardt would make the main investment decisions for the firm, and act as its CEO. Most of the fund's money would come from satisfied clients and family friends.

In 1978 he nearly quit investing entirely, but was persuaded by his partners to take just a year-long sabbatical instead. Ironically, shortly after he returned a year later, he would end up taking sole control from his partners. For the next 16 years, Steinhardt would continue to run money, before finally winding up the fund (which had changed its name to Steinhardt Partners) in 1995. However, he continued to invest his own money and in 2004 he returned to the investment world as chairman of WisdomTree Investments.

From block trading to variant perception

Initially, Steinhardt's fund was known for its involvement in block trading. This involved buying and selling large blocks of shares from large institutions for a discount (and a premium in the case of sales) to the market price, in the hope that they could be unloaded for a profit. Critics argued that SFB then used the market knowledge gained doing this to make money to get ahead of other market participants (for instance, buying in anticipation of a big order). Indeed, Steinhardt himself admitted that he did gain an advantage by this, although he argued that it wasn't against the rules and that it only made a small contribution to overall profits.

Steinhardt claimed that most of his fund's profits came from taking his own positions. His main strategy with these was what he called "variant perception", or what other people would refer to as contrarian investing. He used the money that his fund spent on stock commissions to get huge amounts of information and research from brokers. He would use this to work out the Wall Street consensus about a stock, asset or indeed the entire market. Having established this, he would then do his own research to work out where the market consensus was wrong, and take positions accordingly.

This meant that if he felt that the market was overly negative about something he would buy it and if they were too positive about it he would short it. Most of his trades were short term, and Steinhardt considered himself to be a flexible investor. On several occasions he bought something and made a lot of money when the market moved in his favour, but then felt that the market had moved too much and then took the opposite position.

The not so Nifty Fifty

At the start of the 1970s, growth investing was extremely fashionable. Indeed, investors were particularly interested in the 'Nifty Fifty', a group of around 50 companies – including Kodak, General Electric, Coca-Cola and McDonald's – that were seen as having particularly strong prospects. Because it was assumed that they would keep growing indefinitely, investors were willing to pay high price/earning multiples of around 30–40x for them. Although their sales were indeed growing at a fast rate and he accepted that they were well generally well-run, Steinhardt believed that market sentiment was so positive and valuations so high that the only way the share prices could go was down.

As a result, Steinhardt's fund shorted a large number of these companies in 1972. Initially, Steinhardt's contrarian stance seemed to be mistaken as they kept rising in price. To make matters worse, many of the low-priced value stocks that Steinhardt's fund *did* buy performed poorly. Despite the fund's poor performance that year, and pressure from brokers to cover his positions, Steinhardt maintained his stance. This ended up being rewarded when the stock market crashed over the following two years, with the Nifty Fifty hit particularly badly. Indeed, Polaroid, one of the stocks that Steinhardt had shorted, ended up falling by 91% from its 1972 peak to its 1974 trough.

True to his philosophy, Steinhardt decided by the end of 1974 that the overall market crash had been overdone. He therefore covered his short positions at a huge profit and aggressively invested in stocks, though not in the Nifty Fifty. Again this contrarian stance made him a lot of money when the market did indeed rebound in the mid-to-late 1970s.

Another example of Steinhardt using contrarian investing to make money, this time by going long, was the bond market in the early 1980s. During the late 1970s the Federal Reserve aggressively hiked interest rates in order to combat rampant inflation. Because bond prices decline when interest rates are higher, sky-high rates meant that bond prices were at historic lows. However, Steinhardt believed that the Federal Reserve would have to eventually ease off, because the high interest rates were also damaging the US economy. As a result, his fund borrowed a substantial amount of money to buy five-year US Treasuries.

As with his shorting the Nifty Fifty, the trade did not immediately go in Steinhardt's favour. Indeed, while he started buying Treasuries in early 1981, rates would keep rising until the late summer. This in turn pushed bond prices down further, leading to large losses during the intervening months. However, again he stuck to his guns and refused to sell or reduce his exposure. Of course, when rates started coming down, the value of Treasuries would then start to surge, making him huge profits.

The trades that didn't
work out

Steinhardt did not always follow his own rules, leading to the occasional missed opportunity. Indeed, he would claim that in the run up to Black Monday (19 October 1987), he had become increasingly concerned that the market was overvalued. He was also concerned about the fact that retail investors had started using significant amounts of leverage, another sign of irrational optimism. Finally, he was worried that the increase in derivatives and program trading (a form of arbitrage involving derivatives) had increased potential downside risks.

However, fearful about missing out on gains from a rising stock market, Steinhardt chose not to heed his own warning and continued to maintain large long positions. This meant that when the market plunged over 20% in one day, the fund was fully exposed, costing it an estimated $250m. While the firm would make some money back after the market bounced back, the decision to ignore the warning signs meant that his fund went from being up 45% on the year, to making only 5% (roughly the same as the market during that period).

During the early 1990s Steinhardt would start to sell short-term bonds short and use the money to buy long-term bonds. This strategy worked well, as the Federal Reserve kept interest rates low, allowing him to benefit from the higher yield offered by long-term bonds. Gradually, falling long-term interest rates also boosted the value of the long-term bonds (there is an inverse relationship between bond prices and interest rates), enabling him to make an additional capital gain. After the ERM crisis had died down in late 1993, he bought huge amounts of European bonds as well, allowing himself to be sucked into the market consensus that long-term interest rates would continue to decline.

However, in early 1994 fears about inflation prompted the US Federal Reserve to unexpectedly raise rates instead. This caused bond markets to panic that further rate rises would take place. As a result, both European and US long-term interest rates shot up, pushing down bond prices. The fact that many hedge funds were in a similar position made things worse, because they simultaneously started to unwind their positions, adding fuel to the fire. Because of the huge amount of leverage that Steinhardt had employed, he ended up taking losses of around $1.3bn, causing the value of his hedge fund to fall by around 30% in the space of a few months. Indeed, his losses were so great that it prompted him to retire, though he stayed on until 1995, recouping around $700m of his losses.

Huge returns

Despite these individual mistakes, Steinhardt still managed to have an outstanding track record. Indeed, over the 28 years it was in operation, between 1967 and 1995, Steinhardt's fund made net annual returns of nearly 25% a year. Like other hedge fund managers, Steinhardt charged both an administration and a performance fee, which meant that gross returns were nearer 30%. Even the net returns were nearly double the 13% annual market return for the period.

The success of Steinhardt Partners, which grew from an initial capital base of $7.7m in 1967 to $2.6bn in 1995 (including subsidiary funds), also enabled Steinhardt to amass a fortune, which now stands at $1.04bn according to *Forbes* (as of May 2015). However, his career was not without controversy. In 1994 he had personally to pay over $40m to the Department of Justice to settle claims that he had manipulated the bond market, though Steinhardt would continue to deny the claims, arguing that he had paid to avoid a long legal battle.

Worthwhile, but difficult

Block trading isn't something that ordinary investors can do. However, Michael Steinhardt's track record does show that it is possible to make a lot of money by going against the market consensus, especially when sentiment is at an extreme, as it was with growth stocks in the early 1970s and US bonds in the 1980s. However, it's not enough to be different, you need to be sure that your position is correct. Indeed, Steinhardt points out that many people bet on bonds several years before he did, only to see them go much higher. Similarly, many of the Nifty Fifty companies were good investments, as proved by the fact that some of them bounced back.

Another problem with contrarian investing is that it goes against our human instincts to seek safety in a group. As a result, it's difficult for even the best investor not to follow what everyone else is doing. That's why even Steinhardt ended up going against his own principles on occasion. Steinhardt dealt with his losses after both the 1987 stock market crash and the 1994 bond debacle by selling everything, seeing where he had gone wrong, and then rebuilding his portfolio from scratch.

Even if you are both disciplined enough to be a contrarian, and correct in your timing, you should be prepared for the market to go initially against you. If you want to play a long game, it's vital that you always have enough liquid assets to deal with temporary cash emergencies, so you don't have to sell out of your positions early.

RATING
MICHAEL STEINHARDT

Performance: *Between 1967 and 1995 Steinhardt's fund produced huge returns, enabling him to accumulate a fortune currently estimated at around $1bn. (★★★★★)*

Longevity: *Steinhardt ran money for nearly three decades and continues to be involved in finance. (★★★★★)*

Influence: *Steinhardt is a noted philanthropist and was among the early generation of hedge fund managers. Still, his impact on investing has been limited. (★★)*

Ease of replication: *Steinhardt made leveraged bets, not generally recommended for ordinary investors. He also made some of his money from block trading strategies. (★★)*

Overall rating: 14 out of 20

CHAPTER 5
Benjamin Graham

═══

The Father of Value Investing

Introduction

T HERE ARE A large number of individual investment strategies. However, the two dominant styles are growth and value. Value investing, the art of buying shares at a discount to what they are intrinsically 'worth', was invented by Benjamin Graham. Indeed, Graham's influence on that school of investing is so profound that Warren Buffett (who was himself mentored by Graham) called his famous 1984 survey of the top value managers, 'The Superinvestors of Graham and Doddsville'. Of course, Graham didn't just come up with the theory of value investing – he used it to make a large amount of money for his investors.

Benjamin Graham was born in London in 1894. However, a year later his family moved to New York. Despite having to work several jobs to support his family, he was a star student. However, an administrative mix-up meant that he was rejected for a scholarship to Columbia University, despite doing very well in the entrance exam. After briefly studying at City College of New York, and working for an electrical company, he reapplied and was awarded the scholarship he should have been originally granted. Not only did he complete his degree in two-and-a-half years, but he was offered instructor positions in several departments upon graduation.

Instead, Graham decided that the best career for him was on Wall Street. Recommended by Columbia's dean, he took a job with the bond department of Newburger, Henderson & Loeb. Although he initially started out as a messenger, he rose quickly through the company, becoming partner within six years. However, in 1923 he decided to strike out on his own to manage money for private clients. In 1926 he would found the two investment partnerships with Jerome Newman: the Benjamin Graham Joint Account (later the Graham-Newman Corporation) and the Newman & Graham fund. These would run for over three decades, until his retirement.

Despite choosing Wall Street, Graham didn't abandon academia, teaching a business class at Columbia Business School from 1928 until 1955. Many of his students would become successful fund managers, most notably Warren Buffett (who would also briefly work at Graham-Newman). This course would also become the basis for the 1934 investment classic *Security Analysis* (written with David Dodd). While this book was aimed mainly at financial analysts, he would also write *The Intelligent Investor*, published in 1949, which aimed to bring value investing to a wider audience. The book was a bestseller and popular enough for Graham to revise four times, including shortly before his death in 1976.

Buying value
and smoking cigar butts

In *The Intelligent Investor* Graham dismissed several popular strategies, such as market timing and growth stocks (what he called "long-pull selection"). He viewed attempts to time either individual stock, or the overall market, as "speculation" where the individual had "no real margin for error". Similarly, while he accepted that "a well-chosen company can triple its earnings and quadruple the price of its stock over a period of years", he pointed out that "the long-term future of a company is at best an educated guess". What's more, "if the favourable prospects of a concern are clearly apparent then they are almost always reflected in the stock – *and often overdiscounted*" [emphasis not in the original].

Instead, Graham argued that an investor's best chances came from "bargain purposes", which he defined as "issues which are selling considerably below their true value, as measured by reasonably dependable techniques". Just as growth stocks were frequently overpriced, due to excessive optimism, companies who were doing badly were sometimes underpriced because public sentiment had swung too far against them. Indeed, he argued that "when an individual company or industry begins to lose ground in the economy, Wall Street is quick to assume that its future is entirely hopeless and it should be avoided at any price". Naturally, Graham suggested that this was the best time to buy.

Graham argued that stock prices in general behaved like an eccentric business partner – "Mr Market" – who was willing to offer a certain price for your share of a company. Sometime his views of a firm's value were "plausible and justified by business developments and prospects as you know them". However, at other times "he lets his enthusiasm or fears run away with him, and the value that he proposes seems to you a little short of silly". As a result it made sense to buy into a company when Mr Market's price is low, and then sell out to him "when he quotes you a ridiculously high price".

Graham believed that there were two ways to find out the intrinsic value of a company. One was by using various valuation techniques, usually centred around the future growth of profits. While he accepted that companies with better prospects could demand higher prices, he felt that the investor had a better opportunity of finding bargains with stocks that were trading at lower multiples of prices to earnings (i.e. profits). He particularly liked what he called "cigar butts" – companies which were so disliked by the market that they were trading at a substantial discount to the value of their net assets (assets minus debt).

Indeed, just before he died Graham stated that the only "unfailingly dependable and satisfactory" way to beat the market was to buy into these ultra-cheap companies. This was because "the enormous amount of research now being carried out" meant that "elaborate techniques of security analysis" were no longer generating "sufficiently superior selections to justify their cost".

Graham also believed in what he called the margin-of-safety. Since all human valuation is at best an educated guess, he believed that a company had to be hugely undervalued before it was worth investing in. In many cases it was better to wait until an excellent opportunity came along, rather than settling for one that was merely 'good', just because it happened to be available. This would be taken up by other value investors like Warren Buffett and Seth Klarman.

Graham-Newman Corporation

Graham generally followed both these value strategies in his main fund, the Graham-Newman Corporation. However, it's important to know that he augmented them with two other techniques, convertible arbitrage and merger arbitrage. Merger arbitrage involved buying the shares of a company which was going to be acquired (and selling the shares of the company that was doing the buying) on the expectation that the merger would go through and the price would rise. Convertible arbitrage took advantage of the fact that the price of convertible bonds (bonds which could be converted into shares) were sometimes undervalued compared to the ordinary shares. In this case he would short the shares and buy the convertible bonds.

No records for Graham-Newman's first decade are available. However, Graham himself admitted that although the fund initially did well, it was badly hit by the Wall Street Crash of 1929. Indeed, in the three years following the crash it lost 70% of its value, though this was slightly less than the market as a whole. Graham admitted that part of the problem was that he'd gotten carried away and had bought additional shares with borrowed money to boost returns. As a result of this, Graham and Newman were briefly forced to work for free while the value of their portfolio recovered.

However, for the two decades between the re-founding of the joint account as the Graham-Newman Corporation in 1936 and its winding up in 1956, investors received an average return of around 20% a year (according to Graham in the 1973 edition of *The Intelligent Investor*).

This was mostly in the form of a very high annual dividend, as Graham believed that if the value of the fund got too high it would become hard to find enough good opportunities. Indeed, even by 1956 the fund had net assets of only $6.6m ($57.6m at 2015 prices). This 20% return was far better than the performance of the market as a whole, which returned an annual average of only 10%.

GEICO

Graham's best investment was in the Government Employees Insurance Company (GEICO). At the time GEICO was a fledgling insurance company specialising in selling insurance to government employees. Having made its first profit eight years earlier, earnings were growing at a fast rate. In 1948 the company decided to move from Texas to Washington DC to be closer to its customers. As a result, Cleaves Rhea, a banker who owned 75% of the company, decided to sell his stake.

At the time the insurance industry was reeling from the fact that high inflation meant that policy payouts were outstripping premiums. As a result, the entire sector was extremely unpopular. This meant that Graham-Newman was able to pick up around a third of the company. While Graham was attracted to the company due to the fact that it was trading at a discount to net assets, making it a value investment, he also realised that its use of mail order sales to cut costs and its generally reliable target audience, gave it a competitive advantage over other firms.

Indeed, Graham was so positive about the company that he went against the fund's rule of putting no more than 5% of the fund in each individual investment. Instead, he used a quarter of the fund's assets to acquire half of Rhea's stake in the company (which equated to over a third of the overall company). Because investment companies were only allowed to hold 10% of any one insurance company, the SEC tried to undo the deal. Instead of selling the shares and reinvesting the proceeds, Graham found a way around the rules by giving all of the shares they had acquired directly to their investors as a special dividend.

Both Graham and Newman would continue to hold on to the company long after its price had soared, with Graham serving on GEICO's board of directors from 1948 until 1965. As he would confess in the 1973 edition of *The Intelligent Investor*, he would do so even though "the advance far outstripped the actual growth in profits", which meant that "almost from the start the quotation appeared much too high in terms of the partners' own investment standards".

However, "since they regarded the company, as a sort of 'family business', they continued to maintain a substantial ownership of the shares despite the spectacular price rise". This proved to be a wise decision. Between 1948 and 1956 alone, GEICO's shares would rise tenfold (an annual return of 33%). However, from 1948 to their peak in 1972, their value would rise by over 500 times. Overall, as Graham himself stated, "the aggregate of profits accruing from this single investment-decision far exceeded the sum of all the others realized through 20 years of wide-ranging operations in the partners' specialized fields".

Value matters

A huge amount of research has confirmed Benjamin Graham's belief that investing in shares with low price-to-earnings (p/e) and price-to-book (p/bv) ratios produces higher returns than the overall market. For example, Aswath Damodaran of New York University found that between 1952 and 2010, stocks in the highest price/earnings decile subsequently earned an average of less than 15% a year. In contrast, those with the lowest p/e ratios earned nearly 25% a year. Similarly, between 1927 and 2010 those with the highest p/bv ratios earned only 11%, compared to 17% for the lowest.

There is even evidence that p/e ratios can predict the future direction of the market as a whole. A 2012 study by Joseph Davis of the fund management company Vanguard found a strong negative correlation of 0.38 between the p/e of the US market and subsequent real (inflation-adjusted) 10-year returns between 1926 and 2011. In contrast, variables like predicted GDP growth, previous stock returns, ten-year bond yields or even the growth in profits had little or no explanatory value.

However, Graham's experience of GEICO shows that, while it is important to stick to an investment strategy, it can pay to be flexible on occasions.

RATING
BENJAMIN GRAHAM

Performance: *Graham comfortably beat the market by a huge margin during the last two decades of his partnership with Jerome Newman. However, the value of the fund was badly hit by the Wall Street Crash. It's also important to note that the size of the fund was tiny by modern standards.* (★ ★ ★ ★)

Longevity: *The various investment partnerships between Benjamin Graham and Jerome Newman lasted for over three decades.* (★ ★ ★ ★ ★)

Influence: *Benjamin Graham is regarded as the founder of value investing, thanks to his two books:* Security Analysis *and* The Intelligent Investor. *He would also have a direct influence on a number of other famous investors, most notably Warren Buffett, through his position at Columbia University.* (★ ★ ★ ★ ★)

Ease of replication: *Buying shares with low price-to-earnings ratios, or which are selling below the value of their net assets, is a relatively straightforward strategy, especially given the ready availability of stock-screening tools. There are even exchange-traded funds that allow you to effectively buy a basket of shares with such characteristics.* (★ ★ ★ ★)

Overall rating: 18 out of 20

CHAPTER 6
Warren Buffett

═══

The Elder Statesman of Finance

Introduction

UNSURPRISINGLY, THE WORLD of investing doesn't have many genuine celebrities. Even before the financial crisis in 2008, financiers were more likely to be the object of scorn and suspicion than praise (as George Soros found out). However, Warren Buffett is the exception. Despite being held in the sleepy Midwest town of Omaha, Nebraska, as many as 40,000 people fly down to hear Buffett answer questions at the annual meetings of his holding company, Berkshire Hathaway. These include a large number of overseas investors, including an estimated 3,000 Chinese for the 2016 meeting. Indeed, the popularity of the event has led to it being called "Woodstock for Capitalists".

As well as being a celebrity, Buffett is also considered an elder statesman. After the 11 September terror attacks he was wheeled out to reassure the American public that it was still a good idea to invest in the stock market. Even the blandest of comments that he makes invariably generates headlines. Perhaps the biggest illustration of the respect in which he is held came at the height of the financial crisis in October 2008. At a time when people were seriously questioning whether capitalism, let alone Wall Street, would survive, both presidential candidates suggested that he replace Henry Paulson as Secretary of the Treasury.

So, why is he so popular? Part of his appeal lies in the fact that he is seen as down-to-earth. Despite his billions, he still lives in a suburban house and drives a relatively modest car. He is also recognised as a philanthropist, having pledged in 2006 to give virtually all of his vast personal fortune to charity when he dies. However, the key part of his appeal is his demonstrable ability to consistently beat the stock market for over 50 years, using what many would see as simple 'common sense' investment techniques (though, as shall be explained, things are a little more complicated than that). More than anyone, Buffett's career sends a simple message: *if he can beat the market, so can you.*

From Omaha to Wall Street

Buffett was born in 1930 in Omaha, Nebraska. The son of a stockbroker turned congressman, he exhibited an early entrepreneurial streak, running several businesses while still in school, making enough to buy a farm and invest along with his father in a business. He also was extremely interested in horse racing, becoming a skilled bettor. After studying for two years at Wharton, he finished a degree in business at the University of Nebraska, during which time he started investing in the stock market. Having read both *The Intelligent Investor* and *Security Analysis*, he applied to Columbia Business School, due to the fact that both Benjamin Graham and David Dodd were on the faculty there.

Buffett was a successful student and while doing his MBA he became friendly with both Graham and Dodd. However, he was initially turned down for a job at the Graham-Newman Corporation, despite offering to work for free. Instead he moved back to Omaha and started working as a stockbroker at his father's firm. He also started teaching a night class in investing at the University of Nebraska. After bombarding Graham with investment ideas, Graham relented and hired Buffett in 1954 as an analyst. This job involved doing a huge amount of research on various companies that Graham was thinking of buying, including visiting them.

Buffett enjoyed the work and would later claim that it gave him valuable experience. However, barely more than a year after he had been hired,

Graham told him that he was going to retire from investing. In order to keep the company running after he left, Graham offered to make Buffett co-manager. The catch was that Buffett would have to be subordinate to the son of Graham's partner, Jerry Newman. Deciding that the time had come for him to be in charge, Buffett turned down the offer in favour of returning to Omaha and starting his own partnerships.

Almost as soon as he had returned, Buffett started setting up investing partnerships. The most important of these was Buffett Partners Limited (BPL), which ran from 1956 to 1970. However, by the late 1960s he felt that stocks were too expensive, reducing his chances of getting strong returns and making the 'cigar butt' style of investing (explained in the next section) that he was then using much more difficult. He wound up BPL, recommending that investors invest in bonds instead (which would do very well over the next decade). By this time he was focused on Berkshire Hathaway.

A textile manufacturing firm originally bought as a value investment in 1964, Buffett quickly realised that Berkshire was going nowhere as a textile company due to competition from domestic and foreign plants which could undercut the industry. As a result, he turned it into a holding company for his investments, running it like a hedge fund. Over five decades later Buffett continues to run the fund, although Charlie Munger (who joined in 1978) acts as a senior advisor. Other fund managers also contributed to Berkshire's success by managing the investments of its subsidiaries (such as Lou Simpson for GEICO).

From value to growth

As both a student and disciple of Benjamin Graham, Buffett started out by following Graham's strategy of buying cheap companies. Indeed, BPL would focus on 'cigar-butt' stocks, companies trading at a discount to the value of their net assets (like finding a discarded half-smoked cigar: "though the stub might be ugly and soggy, the puff would be free" to quote Buffett).

Buffett would buy a large stake in these "generals" (as he referred to them) and wait for market sentiment to improve, driving the share prices up to the point at which they could be sold for comfortable profits. However, in some cases, Buffett would use his stake in a company to try and speed up the process of extracting value.

This usually involved separating the firm's underlying business from a much more valuable asset. In a few cases the underlying business proved to be so unprofitable that it had to be wound down. However, in most cases the surplus assets were financial in nature, so the two could be split without damaging operations (or putting anyone out of business). For example, BPL acquired a mapmaking company that owned a large number of bonds and shares (which were not needed to cover any operational expenses or future liabilities). It proved relatively easy to buy out the remaining shareholders, and then split the portfolio from the rest of the business.

Meanwhile around a third of BPL's portfolio was invested in what Buffett called "workouts" (now called merger arbitrage). These were companies that were in the process of being taken over. Usually these companies traded at a discount to the price offered by the company buying them (which itself is almost always at a premium to the price that they were trading at). Buffett would buy these companies on the hope that the rise in price on completion of the deal would more than compensate for the chances of the deal falling through.

However, with Berkshire Hathaway his strategy began to change in two main ways. Firstly, he began to shift away from the idea of buying bargain basement stocks selling below their liquidation value, to stocks that were merely cheap but in companies with solid prospects. Later he would broaden this even further, buying companies that were trading at the same multiples as the rest of the market provided he felt that their long-term prospects were good enough. Of course, Buffett would maintain that he was still following the basic value strategy of buying companies for less than their intrinsic worth. The only difference was that he was now willing to buy a great company that was only trading at a good price.

Of course, Buffett's conversion toward a compromise between growth and value was limited. For instance, he would stay away from technology shares, or anything that seemed overly complicated. Instead, he would focus on companies in easy-to-understand industries, like retailing and insurance, which generated large amounts of cash that could be reinvested in Berkshire. Indeed he placed a great importance on a company having a "moat", his term for an advantage, legal or operational, which prevented competitors from entering and driving down margins. It also allowed the companies he invested in to boost revenue growth by increasing their prices above the rate of inflation.

The other major change was his gradual move away from listed stocks, which would be sold when they became too expensive, towards buying a company outright and then continuing to hold it. Part of the reason for this was that, as the amount of Berkshire's assets grew, Buffett found it increasingly harder to take minority stakes in a small number of mid-sized companies. Buying companies outright allowed him to keep his portfolio relatively concentrated, without limiting himself just to blue chips. Buying insurance companies, one of Buffett's favourite sectors, also had another advantage: the premium money could be reinvested in value shares, earning huge returns before it was eventually needed.

Six decades of success

Whether as a deep value investor or as someone who believed that value and growth were not mutually exclusive, Buffett enjoyed a huge amount of success. From the start of 1957 to the end of 1969, BPL returned an average of just under 30% a year. While the partnership agreement meant that Buffett got a share of the fund's profits, ordinary investors would still get a return equivalent to 23.8% a year, far more than the Dow Jones, which went up by an average of only 7.8%. This meant that $10,000 invested in the fund would have been worth nearly $150,000 13 years later – an impressive return by any measure.

Berkshire Hathaway has also prospered greatly, with shares in the company growing at an annual rate of 20.8% from 1965 to the end of 2015. Again, this is far more than the S&P 500, which only grew by 9.7% during this period. To put this into monetary terms, a $1,000 investment at the start of 1965 would have been worth $15.98m at the end of 2015. Indeed, if you had invested $1,000 in BPL at inception, and then put your money into Berkshire Hathaway stock at the start of 1970, it would now be worth $68.52m. At the time of writing (January 2017) Berkshire Hathaway has a total market capitalisation of $406.9bn. This consistent performance has enabled Buffett to amass a huge fortune, estimated by *Forbes* magazine at $71bn.

Given these impressive figures, it may seem a bit churlish to point out that Buffett's recent performance hasn't been so great. Since the start of 2008, Berkshire Hathaway has trailed the market, returning only 72.4% (up to the end of 2016), compared with 85.5% for the market as a whole. This equates to an annual return of 6.2%, compared with 7.1% for the S&P 500. Buffett has himself accepted that Berkshire's huge size makes it impossible to find the sort of investments that can enable him to replicate the returns that he got earlier.

Picking up
where Graham left off

The one investment that illustrates the evolution in Buffett's style is GEICO. As stated in the previous chapter, the company's price was depressed by the poor performance of the industry in the immediate postwar era. In 1951 a young Warren Buffett, still studying at Columbia, learned that Graham was a GEICO director. He therefore decided to research the company himself, including visiting its offices. After managing to speak to the president's assistant (who would later become the CEO) he realised that the company had a huge amount of potential, even though it was only trading at eight times earnings.

Not only would Buffett invest $10,282 of his own money in the company (roughly two-thirds his net worth), he would write an article about GEICO in a financial journal (*The Commercial and Financial Chronicle*) and recommend it to his clients during his brief period as a stockbroker. However, after the shares sharply increased in value, he made the mistake of selling his stake a year later. While he got $15,259 back from this investment, a return of over 48%, he would miss out on two decades of further gains. Indeed, had he stayed put, he would have multiplied his money eightyfold, more than the return from either Graham-Newman or BPL.

However, Buffett would be given a chance to make up for his mistake in 1976. Thanks to inflation, government regulation and over-expansion, GEICO made its first ever loss in 1975. At the same time a scandal involving misstated profits destroyed the market's confidence in the company. Thanks to all of these factors, combined with a stock market collapse, shares in the company fell from a peak of $61 to just $2. At this point Buffett became interested in the company again as a value investment. His own analysis revealed that the accounting problems weren't as serious as believed, while the firm still had a big advantage over its competitors, through its target market and low-cost selling techniques.

He therefore began to accumulate shares in the company, beginning with a purchase of $23.5m of a mixture of ordinary shares and convertible bonds (bonds that could be converted into shares). He continued to put money into the company over the next four years. By 1980 he owned a third of the company. Unlike in the 1950s, he decided to stick with the company as the price rose, believing that the higher price was more than justified by its growth potential. By 1994 the value of this stake had grown from $105m to $1.68bn, a sixteenfold increase over 14 years, or an annual return of 21.9% from capital gains alone.

Buffett would eventually buy the company outright in 1995. While it is impossible to put a value on how much it is currently worth, one indication of its strength comes from the fact that underwriting revenues have gone up by five times in the last two decades. GEICO's large margins and the fact that the received underwriting revenue (called the float) can effectively be reinvested interest-free, it's safe to conclude that the firm has also been a profitable investment as a private company for Berkshire.

What we can learn from Buffett

Because Buffett's style has gone through such a tremendous evolution, starting out as a deep value investor with BPL and then moving into quality growth, different types of investors take different lessons from his experience. Those who focus on value will point to his earlier successes, using them as an example of how you can make money by buying companies trading below their intrinsic value. In contrast, growth investors claim that his success derived from buying good companies that were able to defend their market positions, and which were therefore able to generate a good cash flow even in bad times.

In truth, despite his forays into growth, Buffett has always been more focused on value. Buffett has himself said that his move towards both growth and the ownership of entire companies (as opposed to individual stocks) was more of a necessity than a free choice. He has also said that given a free rein he would still be following the deep-value approach he used in his BPL years. In a 1999 interview he stated (with just a bit of hyperbole) that "the highest rates of return I've ever achieved were in the 1950s. I killed the Dow. You ought to see the numbers. But I was investing peanuts then. It's a huge structural advantage not to have a lot of money. I think I could make you 50% a year on $1 million."

Still, a lot of Buffett's advice about investment can be applied to any type of investing. For example, he believes that the best way to assess the underlying quality of a business is to focus on the economics rather than the management. As he bluntly puts it, "when a management with reputation for brilliance gets hooked up with a business with a reputation for bad economics, it's the reputation of the business that remains intact."

Buffett has also stated that shareholders should not panic if the prices of shares they own temporarily decline. Just as consumers rejoice if the price of groceries fall because it allows them to buy more food, shareholders should welcome falls in the prices of shares that they own because it enables them to buy more shares. Naturally, such attitudes would have traders like Jesse Livermore pulling their hair out, but for a longer-term investor such a strategy makes sense and could end up increasing returns.

RATING
WARREN BUFFETT

Performance: *Despite a relatively middling performance over the last decade, Berkshire Hathaway has beaten the market by around 5% a year since the mid-1960s, even before taking into account its unfavourable tax position. Buffett's previous partnership did even better.* (★ ★ ★ ★ ★)

Longevity: *Buffett has run various investment partnerships and funds for over six decades.* (★ ★ ★ ★ ★)

Influence: *Buffett's success has made him the public face of Wall Street. At the same time, a lot of fund managers claim to follow his strategy. However, many managers who claim to be inspired by him follow a very different strategy.* (★ ★ ★ ★)

Ease of replication: *Since the 1990s Buffett has moved away from simple stock picking to the extent that the majority of Berkshire's net worth is made up of non-public investments. However, his original strategy of buying a concentrated portfolio of good companies at a cheap price is relatively accessible.* (★ ★ ★)

Overall rating: 17 out of 20

CHAPTER 7
Anthony Bolton

═══

The British Warren Buffett

Introduction

THE SMALLER SIZE of the UK stock market and the traditional British distaste for talking about money means that few British fund managers have the profile of those on the other side of the Atlantic. However, that doesn't mean that they aren't as good. Indeed, Anthony Bolton's track record, both in terms of length of service and performance, puts him among the investment greats. You could even argue that he is a much better model for investors than Warren Buffett, since he stuck to listed companies and kept very closely focused on value, in contrast to Buffett, who has increasingly moved away from listed investments in cheap companies in favour of more conventional blue-chip stocks.

Bolton was born in 1950 and studied business and engineering at Cambridge. Bored with the subject, he was initially undecided on a career, and considered general management. However, at an open day for students given by the industrial conglomerate Procter & Gamble, the organiser admitted to Bolton that both the opportunities and pay were better in finance. A family friend also recommended that he go into the City, arguing that, at the very least, Bolton would pick up useful skills and contacts.

The same family friends also helped Bolton get a job at the investment bank Keyser Ullman. Joining as a trainee, he started out doing relatively menial tasks, including delivering messages and submitting the bank's bid for Treasuries (on one occasion a bid was rejected because he hadn't folded it correctly). Later he moved on to helping various fund managers. However, during the mid-1970s the bank began to experience financial problems, and would eventually collapse in 1975.

By then Bolton had moved to Schlesinger Investment Management, which gave him more direct experience of running money, involving him with several of their funds. As a result of his time at Keyser, a former colleague recruited him to manage Fidelity's Special Situations Fund, beginning in December 1979. He ran the fund for 28 years, stepping down in 2007. He wrote *Investing Against the Tide: Lessons From A Life Running Money* during a brief retirement period, before coming back to run the Fidelity China Special Situations Fund in 2010. In 2014 he retired again, and now has a part-time role mentoring other investment managers.

From stock picker to 'Silent Assassin'

Bolton said that he considered a wide range of factors when buying a share, including: management, company dynamics, financials, the potential for a takeover, valuation and even how its share price had behaved. However, he believed that you could only beat the market if you behaved differently from it. As a result he was primarily a contrarian value investor, looking out for 'cheap', unloved stocks trading at low price/earnings ratios, that the market was overly pessimistic about. He was particularly interested in small firms and 'turnaround situations', troubled stocks that had made big changes to the way that they were run but were still ignored by the market.

Conversely, he was extremely sceptical of companies that everyone was positive about. Indeed, he stated that, while he was open to ideas from external brokers or analysts, if several of them urged him to buy the same share he would stay away. This was because he was worried that such extreme optimism could quickly swing in the opposite direction, turning a stock into a pariah and causing the share price to tank (at which point he might become interested). More generally he felt that it was hard to discover something new about a company that was already covered by a large number of analysts.

To make sure that a firm was worth investing in, Bolton did a lot of bottom-up research on the company's business model and prospects. This included regularly talking to senior management, especially the CEO and head of finance. Indeed, he estimated that he had around 5,000 company meetings for the Special Situations Fund alone in the 20 years since 1987. Bolton believed in looking at as many companies as possible, on the principle that the more he viewed, the greater the chance of finding a bargain. Even when the number of individual shareholdings began to increase, he still believed in spending most of his time on what he called "offensive research", which meant looking for new opportunities.

Of course, this didn't mean that he neglected those companies that he had invested in. Indeed, while he was always primarily a stock picker, the increasing size of his funds forced him to become more and more involved in the governance and strategy of the various companies that they held. This was particularly noticeable in the smaller firms, where Fidelity was frequently the largest or second largest investor. In several cases it proved difficult to sell large numbers of shares in a short time without adversely moving the price. As a result, it was frequently more economical to first try and change an underperforming company from inside.

Perhaps the most well-known example of Bolton's activism was where two independent television companies, Carlton Communications and Granada, merged to form ITV Plc. With Fidelity a major shareholder in both companies, Bolton's support for the deal played a key role in it going through. However, he was opposed to the idea of Michael Green of Carlton Communications becoming ITV's chief executive in 2003, and spearheaded the opposition to him. The success of this campaign earned him the nickname of the 'Silent Assassin'.

Three decades of success — both at home and abroad

The above strategies seemed to work spectacularly for Bolton. £1,000 invested in the Fidelity Special Situations Fund in December 1979 would have been worth £1.45m by the time he stepped down 28 years later. This equates to an average 19.5% return annually, compared with 13.5% for the FTSE during the same period. This wasn't just a case of one or two good years accounting for much of the difference: Bolton outperformed the market in 19 of the 26 years between 1980 and the end of 2005. Although the fund was split into two halves in 2006, the UK part (which Bolton managed) was still worth £3bn in December 2007.

While the Special Situations Fund focused almost exclusively on the UK, Bolton's superb track record extended to other markets. Between December 1985 and the end of 2002, he was also the lead manager for the Fidelity European Fund. While this followed a similar investment strategy to the main fund, it covered the rest of Europe. Over the 17 years of Bolton's tenure, it returned 19%, with a £1,000 growing into just under £20,000. Given that the wider European market returned only 10% during this period, Bolton beat the index by a higher amount than with his UK fund.

Bolton's best calls

Antony Bolton's most successful investment was in Securicor, which was the largest holding in his portfolio during the late 80s and much of the early-to-mid 90s. While its main business was providing security, Bolton realised that the real value of the company lay in its co-ownership of the pioneering mobile network Cellnet, which it co-founded with BT in 1985. Securicor's remaining stake in Cellnet was finally bought for £3.15bn at the height of the tech boom in 1999. While Bolton sold his shares in Securicor well before then, between 1989–96 Securicor soared in value.

As well as being correct on specific stocks, Bolton also made some shrewd sectoral choices, avoiding the technology sector at the height of the bubble in the late 1990s. This meant that while the wider market fell 6% during 2000, his fund made a very impressive 25%, outperforming the market by a whopping 31%. Of course, after the collapse in technology stocks in 2000–2, many of them became so cheap that Bolton, ever the contrarian, picked them up at bargain prices, enabling Fidelity Special Situations to do very well in 2003, 2004 and 2005.

Bolton's turbulent Chinese experience

However, Bolton did make one notable misstep. In 2009 he decided to make a return to fund management, launching an investment trust, the Fidelity China Special Situations Fund, in April 2010. The idea was to apply Bolton's value-driven, contrarian approach to the Chinese market, in the hope that strong growth and the rise of the consumer economy would help smaller companies. Bolton's previous track record meant that investors flocked to put money into it, which enabled it to initially raise £460m. This was despite the fact that it charged investors an additional performance-related fee in addition to a management charge of 1.5%.

Initially this investment trust did very well, with the share price surging by 20% in a matter of months. Sadly, for Bolton, this didn't last. Starting in the autumn of 2010, and lasting for a year, the value of the fund's portfolio plunged. As a result, the investors – initially willing to pay a premium for the shares – panicked. The trust's shares were sent spiralling downwards in value. The peak-to-trough fall was 40%. Bolton claimed that he had been misled by the management of several companies that he had invested in, and blamed the general downturn in the market (which had also fallen but by much less).

Despite his explanations, Bolton received a huge amount of criticism in the press, especially for the fact that the fund had borrowed money in order to boost returns (which magnified the losses). He would eventually step down at the end of March 2014, just under four years after he had started the fund. However, even then his performance wasn't that bad. Indeed, while the fund posted a total return of only 6.3%, the overall market fell by 5.7% during the same period. Indeed, the value of the portfolio grew by 18.6% (because an investment trust is traded on the stock market, its share price and the value of its shares usually differ by a small amount).

The importance of value investing

Bolton's career demonstrates that small-cap and value-based investing can be a powerful tool, especially if you have the ability to spot companies that are about to make a comeback, thereby benefiting from both an increase in earnings and a change in sentiment. However, it's important to note that Bolton didn't just blindly buy companies that were trading at low multiples of price/earnings. Instead he carried out a lot of research to enable him to judge whether the companies that he was considering were genuine bargains, as opposed to companies that were cheap because they had serious problems.

Of course, doing such research is much harder for ordinary investors who won't be able to meet with management and may have a very limited time to scrutinise companies. However, regulatory changes and the rise of technology means that most listed companies now put a huge amount of information on the internet. This usually includes annual reports and presentations to investors. There are also a large number of stock filters available on the internet that can help you focus on cheap stocks that may be potential bargains. Avoiding sectors that are overhyped, or receive a disproportionate amount of press attention, is another way to help you maximise your time.

However, Bolton's experience in China is a cautionary tale, proving that emerging markets are not risk-free. Indeed, in some countries accounting standards and corporate governance are so poor that even professionals struggle to spot fraud. As a result, unless you really know what you are doing, or are prepared to deal with a lot of volatility, you should really consider avoiding direct investment in some of the more exotic countries. One alternative to trying to pick individual shares is to find a country- (or region-) specific exchange-traded fund that allows you to invest in a broad basket of stocks.

RATING
ANTHONY BOLTON

Performance: *Between 1979 and 2007, Bolton's fund beat the market by over 6% a year. While his brief Chinese experience was much less successful, he still managed to beat the market.* (★ ★ ★ ★ ★)

Longevity: *Bolton has been involved in fund management for over four decades.* (★ ★ ★ ★ ★)

Influence: *During his later years as a fund manager, Bolton had a very high profile. However, he hasn't had a huge amount of influence on investing as a whole.* (★ ★)

Ease of replication: *Bolton's value strategy is relatively easy to follow. However, it required a huge amount of research. Except in a few circumstances, ordinary investors are unlikely to have much ability to use their holdings to influence a company.* (★ ★)

Overall rating: 14 out of 20

CHAPTER 8
Neil Woodford

≡≡≡

The Top Current Value Manager
in Britain

Introduction

WITH ANTHONY BOLTON'S retirement from directly managing money, Neil Woodford has taken over the mantle of Britain's most well-known fund manager. Like Bolton, he's amassed a long record of extraordinary returns, and follows a similar investment philosophy of buying undervalued shares and holding them until they rise in price. Indeed, his reputation is such that his decision to leave Invesco in 2014 made the headlines. It also saw investors dump the fund that he worked for and queue up to invest with the company that he founded (and is CEO of): Woodford Investment Management.

Since then he has stayed very much in the public eye, launching several additional funds. Recent high-profile moves include the decision to scrap bonuses at his firm in favour of flat salaries. His belief that the financial sector isn't doing enough to help turn scientific discoveries into tangible businesses has led him to become a big advocate for what he terms "patient capital". This is essentially venture capital investing over a much longer time frame than the three-to-five-year period over which most venture capital firms expect to get a return. Despite this, his biggest contribution to the world of investment has been his performance as a fund manager.

From flying planes to
City high-flyer

Born in 1960, Woodford studied economics and agricultural economics at Exeter University. Initially, his dream was to be in the Royal Air Force. However, his reaction times weren't good enough to get him accepted into the training programme for fighter pilots (though they were good enough for the slightly lesser role of navigator). He was also rejected by British Airways. As a result, he decided to put his economics degree to good use by getting a job in the City. However, in 1981 the economy was in recession and jobs were hard to find, so he started out with an admin job at a commodities firm, which had previously been filled by those who left school at 16.

He was quickly able to get on to the graduate track at the Dominion Insurance Company, ending up as the assistant of one of their fund managers. This would give him a first taste of the world of money management. Over the next eight years Woodford climbed the corporate ladder with a series of bigger roles at various financial firms, such as Reed Insurance, TSB and the insurance company Eagle Star. At the same time he complemented his practical experience with postgraduate studies in finance at London Business School.

He came to realise that pension and insurance companies made most of their investment decisions by committee. This meant that, no matter how high he climbed, he would have extremely limited autonomy to make the sort of contrarian investment decisions that are needed to significantly outperform the market. He therefore decided to take up a position at Perpetual (now Invesco Perpetual), then a relatively unknown fund management company, in early 1988. Coming in the wake of the 1987 crash, which had seen stock markets across the world plummet in a matter of days, this was seen by many of his friends and colleagues as an eccentric move.

However, he would thrive in his new environment, staying there for 26 years, until 2014. During this time he would be put in charge of multiple funds, beginning with Invesco Perpetual High Income (which he ran from

February 1988 to March 2014). Other funds included: Invesco Perpetual Income (1990–2014), the Edinburgh Investment Trust (2008–2014) and SJP Strategic Managed (2010–2014). Despite this success, he became disenchanted with the short-term attitudes of the City, and wanted more autonomy to pursue his interests. Scrapping plans to retire, he decided instead to leave Invesco Perpetual and strike out on his own.

At the moment, Woodford Investment Management runs three funds, all managed by Woodford himself. The CF Woodford Equity Income Fund is his main fund and very similar in goals and style to the Invesco Perpetual High Income. The CF Woodward Income Focus Fund places more weight on delivering regular dividends. Finally, the Patient Capital Trust, a listed investment trust, aims to invest in unlisted (and some listed) small-cap technology companies, especially those spun out of universities, with the aim of holding them for longer periods than other private-equity or venture funds.

Value investing for the long term

With the exception of the Patient Capital Trust, Woodford has been at heart a value investor, buying shares in companies that he thinks are undervalued, and avoiding those that he sees as too expensive. He also deliberately avoids market timing or elaborate attempts to forecast the direction of the economy. Instead of keeping large amounts of cash in his portfolio, in anticipation of future buying opportunities, he is almost fully invested in shares, arguing that, over the medium run, a good, fundamentally oriented value investor should be able to overcome any temporary market blips.

However, Woodford's type of value investing is much closer to that of Warren Buffett, whom he cites as a major influence, than Benjamin Graham. Instead of buying the very cheapest stocks, with a view to dumping them immediately after they rise in price so that he can dive back into the bargain bin, he likes to focus on good-quality companies that he expects to do well over at least a three-to-five-year period. He strongly believes that, "by taking a long-term perspective … fund managers can truly add value" and approves of Buffett's observation that "if you aren't willing to hold a stock for ten years then you probably shouldn't even think of owning it for ten minutes".

Of course, this longer-term approach hasn't stopped him from selling holdings that have become too expensive or have developed serious structural problems. However, on average he has consistently held shares for much longer periods than his rivals, and with a lower portfolio turnover. He estimates that his "average investment holding period during [his] career has been between five and seven years, although it has been higher during particular periods".

Another key element of Woodford's approach is the emphasis on portfolio concentration. At the time of his departure from Invesco, the Equity High Income Fund's top ten holdings accounted for slightly more than half the portfolio. Similarly, while the CF Woodford Equity Income Fund currently has holdings in over 100 companies, the top ten holdings again account for over half the portfolio.

Like Bolton, he has also been an activist investor, most notably using his holdings in the engineering and defence firm BAE to block a proposed merger with the European aerospace company EADS. "If I am asking investors to trust me with their money, I will not be an absentee landlord or invest and hope for the best," he argues. Of course, he accepts that "you can't ever get full transparency with a business". However, "you can still engage with it and work as hard as you can to find out whether a business is actually doing what it says it is doing".

Strong performance

An investment of £10,000 in Invesco High Income Perpetual – Woodford's main fund – when he joined in 1988 would be worth £253,490 in 2014.

This works out at an annual return of 13.2%, significantly higher than the 9.3% that the FTSE All-Share returned during the same period. It's important to note that Woodford didn't rest on his laurels. During the last ten years of Woodford's tenure, the fund beat the market by around 5% a year, coming top out of 51 similar UK income funds. These returns combined with capital flooding into the account meant that by the time Woodford announced his departure in October 2013, the fund held around £33bn in assets.

In its two-and-a-half years of operation, the Woodford Equity Income Fund has experienced several ups and downs. After an initial surge in price, it had a disappointing 2016, increasing only slightly in a year when the FTSE surged by 16.8%. However, overall it has still beaten the market, returning a cumulative total of 25.6% since it started in June 2014 (as of 31 January 2017), compared with 16.2% for the FTSE. As a result, the amount of assets under management has increased to £9.3bn.

Skipping down Tobacco Road

During the late 1990s, Neil Woodford made two momentous investment decisions that would seal his reputation. Firstly, he would stay away from technology stocks, as he believed them to be too expensive. At the time, his failure to jump on the technology bandwagon seemed like a big mistake as those shares surged, leading him to lag the stock market for several years. While his employers stuck with him, he admitted that had the technology crash happened six months later, even they would have had to dump him. Of course, when the crash did occur, the fact that he had avoided them enabled him to retake pole position from his competitors.

Secondly, around the same time, Woodford would heavily invest in tobacco companies. This seemed like the ultimate contrarian move, since they were being forced to settle a series of government lawsuits that ultimately resulted in them having to pay the government billions of dollars in healthcare costs.

Meanwhile there was a general perception that declining sales in developed countries meant that they had little future. In contrast, Woodford realised that the settlement ironically ensured the government had a stake in their continued survival.

Meanwhile, he also grasped that continued economic growth in emerging markets would lead to a rapid increase in cigarette consumption in those countries, which would keep global sales growing. This proved to be an extremely wise decision as the price of British American Tobacco (BAT), which would become one of his fund's core holdings, rose twelvefold from 250p in 2000 to over £31 by the time he left Invesco. Taking dividends into account, this amounts to an annual return of over 20% a year. It's therefore not surprising that Woodford has stated that one of his biggest regrets was that he didn't buy even more tobacco shares.

Missed opportunity with banks

Despite his success avoiding the technology bubble, Woodford would have a more mixed experience with the banking sector. In 2005 banks were doing extremely well, with a surging housing market leading to a surge in lending. However, Woodford decided that the banks were taking on too much debt and they would be badly exposed during any economic downturn. He therefore dumped his holdings in bank shares and switched to defensive companies, such as utilities. This pessimistic approach seemed to be vindicated when the housing market did indeed crash, both prompting an economic recession and causing a global financial crisis.

Woodford's low exposure to financial stocks cushioned the blow for his investors during the financial crisis. The problem is that he continued to be downbeat on the banking sector for the next five years, believing that the problems that had caused the crash hadn't been properly dealt with.

This meant that his fund didn't benefit from the huge recovery in bank shares that followed the round of bailouts and money printing in Britain and America. Combined with his defensive posture, this ensured that his fund would end up trailing the market during the five years from the end of 2008.

Upsides (and downsides) of value investing

On one level Neil Woodford's career is another illustration that a contrarian value-focused approach, if properly applied, can deliver large returns. However, it does illustrate some of the downsides to such a strategy, especially for fund managers who have to consistently beat an index. While he managed to survive long enough to take advantage of the change in market direction that occurred in 2000, others were not so fortunate, with Tony Dye of Phillips & Drew being fired almost on the day that the bubble started to burst (although Dye had put large amounts of his fund into cash rather than merely avoiding tech stocks).

Woodford's decision to invest in tobacco stocks raises the question of how far you should let ethical concerns determine your choice of investments. Woodford has defended his investments on the grounds that many other sectors (such as arms manufacturers) are just as problematic from a moral point of view but don't raise the same objections. He also argues: "I am not paid to exercise my moral judgements in my portfolio. I am paid to exercise my investment judgements – and invest purely on what I believe are the best investment opportunities for my clients". Indeed he thinks that "the tobacco sector still looks structurally undervalued and is, therefore, an appealing investment".

The good news for socially concerned investors is that there seems to be an academic consensus that traditional ethical investing has no serious negative impact on returns. For example, a 2002 study by Rob Bauer comparing the performance of 103 ethical funds with 4,384 normal funds in Germany, the UK and the US between 1994 to 2004 found evidence of both higher and lower returns that were mostly statistically insignificant. At the same time, the main socially responsible indices have performed roughly the same as their more mainstream equivalents.

Indeed, a study by Alexander Kempf and Peer Osthoff of the University of Cologne found that actively searching out companies that behave particularly ethically, rather than just excluding certain sectors, actually boosted returns. They found that a strategy of ranking US companies by their socially responsible behaviour, and then buying the most ethical and selling the least ethical, would have produced an excess return of nearly 9% between 1992–2004.

RATING
NEIL WOODFORD

Performance: *During his time at Invesco, Woodford beat the market by just under 4% a year. While his new funds have only been operating for a relatively short period, his main one continues to beat the market.*
(★ ★ ★ ★)

Longevity: *Woodford has been running money for nearly three decades. (★ ★ ★ ★ ★)*

Influence: *Woodford has achieved recognition for his investing skill. However, like Anthony Bolton, his contribution to the field of investing has been limited. (★ ★)*

Ease of replication: *Woodford's concentrated value strategy is relatively straightforward for investors to replicate, although his recent moves into patient capital are much less so. (★ ★ ★)*

Overall rating: 14 out of 20

CHAPTER 9
Philip Fisher

═══

The Inventor of Growth Investing

Introduction

A s WE'VE DISCUSSED, value investors believe that it's hard to be certain about the future, so you should try and buy stocks that seem cheap relative to their earnings, dividends and net assets. In contrast, growth investors think that it is impossible to determine the true value of a company, and that if you pick good quality companies that can keep growing their earnings the share price will look after itself.

This debate is still unresolved. While the evidence suggests that value may have the edge over the long run, there have been periods when growth shares have done much better. Indeed, over the past decade growth has outperformed, both in the US and globally. For example, Vanguard's index measuring growth stocks has beaten that covering value stocks by just under 3% a year. Similarly, in the past ten years the MSCI World Growth Index has beaten the MSCI World Value Index by around 2%. If Benjamin Graham is regarded as the intellectual force behind value investing, Philip Fisher was one of the first to make the case for focusing on growth.

Career break proved a hidden blessing

Born in 1907 in San Francisco, Fisher did a degree in economics at Stanford before starting an MBA at its newly founded business school. Eager to take advantage of the stock market boom that was taking place, he would leave the course after only a year. Ironically, his later success meant that he would be invited back to teach a course on investing to MBA students between 1960–62. After a brief stint in the analysis department of a local bank and at a stock exchange firm, he decided to set up his own investment firm, Philip Fisher & Company, in 1931, enjoying moderate success.

During the second world war, Fisher took a desk job in the US Army Air Corps (later the US Air Force). While this meant that he had to temporarily suspend his investing career, he later believed that it was a blessing in disguise. With plenty of spare time, Fisher was able to analyse his own performance and see where there was room for improvement. He realised that most of his profits came from buying companies and holding them, rather than trying to buy shares when they were cheap and selling them when they were dear.

After the war he would return to the investment advisory business until he retired in 1999 (he died in 2004). Since it was a private fund that only served a small number of key clients, Fisher didn't publish any data on his performance. However, he was generally acknowledged to be an extremely successful investor, managing around $500m at his peak. The thing that ensured he would have a huge influence on investing is his series of books, most notably his bestselling 1958 book, *Common Stocks and Uncommon Profits*. His other investment books, *Paths to Wealth Through Common Stocks* (1960) and *Conservative Investors Sleep Well* (1975) would also be successful, and have been cited by other legendary investors, including Warren Buffett.

Finding fast-growing companies

Fisher believed that "the greatest investment reward comes to those who by luck or good sense find the occasional company that over the year can grow in sales and profits far more than industry as a whole". In practice this meant well-run companies with huge growth potential. Provided a stock met this criteria, it was worth holding on to, irrespective of any fluctuation in price. You should be willing to put up with periods when the share price goes nowhere, or declines (indeed Fisher would wait at least three years before selling a company). Conversely, he believed that you should not be tempted to cash in simply because the price had gone up.

While Fisher liked firms that consistently grew their dividends, he preferred them to keep the yield low and to reinvest profits in the company. In his view this allowed them to keep growth rates high. He also argued that investors should spend less time focusing on quantitative data in annual reports, and more time on what he termed "scuttlebutt". This "scuttlebutt" meant qualitative information about the quality of a firm's management, operations and products, not 'hot tips' or inside information (which is of course illegal to take advantage of anyway).

Indeed, he would come up with a list of 15 key things that investors should look for. These can be divided into three groups: strategy, operations and management. Firstly, a company needed to have a strategy that would allow it to keep growing for a long period of time, and to move into new markets when existing markets matured. It also needed to have strong profit margins and a plan for protecting them from the ravages of competition and inflation. A competitive advantage that enabled it to stay ahead of its competitors (like economies of scale or patents) was also extremely useful, as was a long-run approach to profits.

In terms of operations, Fisher felt that the two key parts of a company were its research-and-development department and its salesforce. This was because researchers would develop the products that would enable it to keep growing. However, few products were so outstanding that they automatically sold themselves, which meant that the company needed a salesforce that was at the top of its game. Good labour relations were also vital to keep the workforce productive, ensure loyalty to the company and avoid strikes that could disrupt operations. Strong cost control and balance sheet capacity, including the ability to borrow additional money if needed, would also ensure the financial health of the company.

Finally, Fisher advised investors to pay attention to the quality of a company's management. This included good relations between the various executives, and a strong team that enabled the top executives to delegate responsibility. He also thought that it was imperative that the management behaved in an honest fashion. One possible red flag was if they dealt with bad news by trying to hide it from investors. At the very least, such behaviour indicated that they were unprepared for failure, itself troubling. However, it could also suggest that they didn't care about their shareholders.

Texas Instruments and Motorola

One of Fisher's best investments was the semiconductor company Texas Instruments (TI). He first bought into the company in 1955, and then bought a bigger amount a year later after the management, who were also its major shareholders, sold a chunk of shares in 1956 (though he had first learned about it two years earlier). He believed that the industry had a huge growth potential, which would enable TI to keep increasing profits. However, he also liked the way that the company was run, particularly the fact that it put a lot of effort into further research and had plans for strengthening its sales organisation. He also liked the fact that it had a strong government and military electronics business.

At the time many brokers recommended that their clients should sell it, on the grounds that the company was too expensive, trading at around 20× earnings. They were also worried by the fact that the company's executives were selling and that bigger firms could enter the market. However, Fisher believed that these concerns were exaggerated. He noted that the managers were selling for legitimate reasons (most of their net wealth was invested in the company and they wanted to both diversify and plan for their children's inheritance). He also believed that TI's status as the lowest-cost producer would help it deal with any competition.

Fisher not only bought into the company, but tipped it as an example of the type of growth company that people should buy into in various editions of *Common Stocks and Uncommon Profits*, and his later works. It would also become a major part of the portfolios that he managed for his clients. Unfortunately, as he ruefully pointed out in an interview, one of his major clients insisted on selling their shares in TI after it initially soared in price, on the expectation that they would be able to buy them back more cheaply. However, while the shares did eventually fall back a few years later, they never reached the price at which the client had sold them.

Fisher's advice to hang on would ultimately be proved right. Indeed, prices rose so much that the stock split on several occasions (a split is where a single share is exchanged for two new shares in order to keep the price of a single share affordable). By the time the share price peaked in 2000, a year after Fisher's retirement, it had increased over 1,500 times its level in 1956. This meant that those who had invested in 1956 would have made an annual return of 18%, even before any dividend reinvestment.

If Texas Instruments demonstrates the strengths of Fisher's strategy, Motorola shows its weaknesses. Fisher started buying Motorola shares in 1955, and would keep large holdings in the company until his death in 2004. Although he initially heard about it from another investor, he only decided to invest after visiting the company's plant and being impressed by the management. This initially proved to be a very successful investment, going up 20× in two decades, compared with seven times for the market. However, from the 1980s onwards it would slightly lag the market (though if you had sold at the height of the tech bubble in 2000 you would have done much better).

Companies for all seasons

The idea of a share portfolio that you can hold for years on end without having to make many changes or do anything other than watch prices soar, is alluring to many time-poor investors. Fisher's career shows that it is possible to find such a group of shares.

However, building such a collection is a little more complex (and time-consuming) than just picking those that have gone up the most, or even ones which have strong sales growth in the past year (indeed Texas Instruments's earnings had been previously flat). Instead, it involves a very long and detailed analysis that takes a long-term perspective. Therefore 'Fisher-style growth investing' only suits those who are willing to make a large initial investment of time in order to save effort later on.

It's also important to note that Fisher was lucky to end his career near the peak of the technology bubble. Indeed, had an investor bought into either Motorola or Texas Instruments in 1999, they would still be looking at a loss three decades on. This suggests that even the best stocks can get too expensive. Similarly, there comes a time when even the most innovative companies can lose their edge, get so big that they become unwieldy, or are made obsolete by a new technology.

Because companies that can outperform for decade after decade are very rare, Fisher believed in limiting the number of individual stocks that you hold in your portfolio. While he accepted that there were some benefits to diversification, he argued that these quickly diminished the more stocks that you held. He also argued that one of the disadvantages of putting stocks in many different baskets was that "a lot of the eggs do not end up in really attractive baskets". It also meant that investors put money into companies that they knew little about.

Fisher argued that, provided the companies that you buy are not in the same industry, and had multiple businesses (allowing them to still make money if one part of the business had a bad year), you could get away with five different large companies (limiting each investment to a fifth of the portfolio). Even in the case of smaller, more volatile companies that were in the early stages of growth, you could get away with ten firms. In any case, he felt that it was not just pointless, but counterproductive, for investors to own shares in more than 25 companies at any one time.

This position may seem rather extreme. Indeed, there are few people who would suggest that five is an acceptable number to have. However, the evidence suggests that the benefits of diversification diminish rapidly. A famous 1977 study by Edwin Elton and Martin Gruber found that the average standard deviation of a US share was 49.3%. This means that nearly a third of the time its value would go up or down by more than half. Increasing the portfolio to ten shares would cut this in half to 24%. However, a 20-share portfolio would still have a standard deviation of 21.2%, while having 1,000 shares would only cut risk from 21.7% to 19.2%.

RATING
PHILIP FISHER

Performance: *Philip Fisher didn't run any public funds so there aren't any records of how he did. However, the general consensus is that he managed to make his clients a lot of money.* (★★★★)

Longevity: *Fisher was involved in the market for several decades.* (★★★★★)

Influence: *Philip Fisher has been credited with inventing growth investing. Even many value investors, like Warren Buffett, say that he has been a tremendous influence on them.* (★★★★★)

Ease of replication: *Philip Fisher's idea of identifying companies that can produce decades of above-average returns, requires a bit of research. But the idea is that once you create a portfolio, it will require minimal maintenance.* (★★★)

Overall rating: 17 out of 20

CHAPTER 10
T. Rowe Price

The Pragmatic Growth Investor

Introduction

P HILIP FISHER REPRESENTS the purest (or most extreme) form of growth investing: just buy shares in great companies whatever the price and then keep holding them. However, as discussed in the previous chapter, there are several problems with this approach. The biggest is that few companies are able to keep growing for any extended period of time. Indeed, a 2003 study by Louis Chan of the University of Illinois found that between 1951–2008 only 6.3% of listed American firms were able to maintain above-median sales growth for five consecutive years. Fewer than 1% were able to do it for ten years.

Even if companies keep outperforming, their price can simply get too high, as investors found out the hard way during the peak of the technology bubble around the turn of the millennium. As a result, most modern growth investors tend to follow the example of Thomas Rowe Price Jr. Although a contemporary of Fisher, Price represented a more pragmatic school of growth investing, one which took a more immediate perspective and didn't completely discount the role of dividends or valuation in the stock-selection process. His brand of growth investing also placed great emphasis on the right time to sell a stock.

From chemistry to
money management

Thomas Rowe Price Jr was born in 1898 near Baltimore, Maryland. The son of a local doctor, Price graduated with a chemistry degree from Swarthmore College. However, after spending several years working as an industrial chemist at DuPont, he switched careers, becoming a stockbroker with Mackubin, Goodrich and Company (now Legg Mason). While he enjoyed investing, he felt that the brokerage model, whereby he was paid a commission based on the number of trades he executed, meant that his interests weren't fully aligned with those of his clients.

In 1937 he took the decision to start his own wealth advisory firm, Price Associates, along with fellow managers Charles Shaeffer and Walter Kidd. This meant that he was now paid a percentage of the assets that he had under management, allowing him to offer much more objective advice. Indeed, one of his favourite sayings, and one which Price Associates (now T. Rowe Price) still likes to quote on its website, is "if we do well for the client, we'll be taken care off". He would also write a series of articles for *Barron's* magazine on investing. These were published in 1939 as a pamphlet with the title *Picking Growth Stocks*.

While Price Associates was successful just serving clients, Rowe Price decided to found the T. Rowe Price Growth Stock Fund in 1950. One of the first mutual funds, it was initially created as a way to help existing clients set up investment funds for their children. His decision not to impose an initial sales charge on new money (referred to as a 'load') meant that the fund became extremely popular, especially during the 1960s when growth stocks were in fashion. In 1960, Price Associates launched the New Horizons Fund, which primarily focused on smaller, riskier growth companies.

However, as the market advanced, Price became increasingly worried that growth stocks were overvalued, especially against a background of rising inflation. As a result, he started to make public warnings, culminating in a pamphlet entitled *The New Era for Investors*. This argued that investors should switch over to natural resources stocks, as well as traditional inflation hedges such as gold and real estate. While the firm would eventually follow his advice, setting up the New Era fund in 1969, which invested in gold and energy stocks, Price was so disillusioned with the market excesses that he retired in 1966, and four years later sold all his shares in the company that he had founded.

Between 1970 and his death in 1983, Price would keep in touch with the market by managing the portfolios of friends and family. He would also make occasional comments in the press on the state of the market.

Growth – but not at any price

T. Rowe Price's approach to stock picking shared a lot of similarities with that of the other legendary growth investor, Philip Fisher. Both believed that the best way to make money in the stock market was from buying into companies that could grow their earnings over at least the short and medium term. Price also liked firms with a technological advantage, less competition, safety from regulation and low labour costs. Similarly, he felt that poor management and market saturation could pose major threats to a firm's continued growth, and should prompt an investor to consider selling.

However, while Fisher was very much focused on a bottom-up approach, which treated each company as an individual, Price felt that you should focus on the industry that they were in. As a result, he primarily searched for companies in fast-growing sectors of the economy. He believed that these could either be completely new sectors or industries that had been given a new lease of life by a new invention or development elsewhere, although he accepted that speciality companies expanding into new areas were also worth considering. As a result, he frequently bought shares in multiple companies in the same industry.

Since Price was also sceptical of long-term forecasting, arguing that it was impossible to know what would happen in the distant future, he wanted the companies in his portfolio to have a track record of strong earnings growth in the immediate past. He accepted that year-to-year results could vary because of the economic cycle. However, he insisted that their earnings had to show an upward trend. One rule of thumb that he quoted in *Picking Growth Stocks* was that the average earnings of the last five years should be 50% higher than those of the five years before that.

Another metric that he closely followed was return on invested capital. He argued that a high return on invested capital was indicative of either a dominant market position, or at least that a company was making an efficient use of its capital. However, if the return on capital started to decline, this suggested that the firm was under increased competitive pressure, since competition should theoretically drive down returns to the cost of capital. It could also indicate that the company was artificially boosting growth by making unproductive investments that would not cover their costs.

Price also felt that "one of the major objectives of investors who buy common stocks is income", and that growth stocks were not exempt from this. As a result, his ideal companies were those that were regularly increasing their dividends, or had a reasonable chance of doing so in the future. Price acknowledged that dividend payments were more of a problem for some, especially fast-growing companies, while firms that had only recently been listed weren't able to pay dividends at all. However, he felt that at a minimum, firms had to have plans for paying out some sort of dividend in the near future otherwise they weren't worth investing in.

Perhaps Price's biggest disagreement with Fisher was the former's belief that valuation should play a role in investment decisions. In contrast to Fisher's growth-at-any-cost strategy, Price felt that even the best firms would struggle to meet expectations once they had risen to a certain level. While he had no hard-and-fast formula for how a stock should be valued, he felt that companies with a very low earnings yield (i.e. a high price/earnings ratio) were rarely good value. This was especially the case when interest rates were higher.

Strong track record

The Growth Stock Fund, T. Rowe Price's main fund, did well during its first two decades of operation. Indeed, between 1950 and the end of 1972 (two years after he severed all ties with the company), $10,000 invested in the fund would have grown into $228,370, an average return of 14.5%. While the market also grew strongly during this period, the equivalent sum put into the market would only have grown into $179,200 (an average of 13.4%). Price's strong performance meant that by 1966, the year of his retirement from fund management, his firm controlled around $1.5bn worth of assets (equivalent to $11.5bn at 2015 prices).

He did even better when managing the private accounts of specific clients. Indeed, the stock selections in one family account that he managed from 1934 to the end of 1972 grew by an average of 16% (excluding taxes). This was noticeably better than the wider market, which could only manage to produce an annual return of 11.4% during the same period. While Price didn't provide any figures for his performance after 1972, his decision to ditch growth stocks in favour of gold and energy companies, before returning to growth companies after the crash of 1974, made him a lot of money.

High-flying stocks

One example that Price would use to illustrate the gains from growth investing was his investment in the aircraft industry in the mid-1930s. At the start of 1934 he felt that aviation was a fast-growing sector that would benefit from both an increase in civilian demand and global military rearmament, in what would prove to be the run up to the second world war. He therefore bought shares in five aircraft companies: Curtiss-Wright, Douglas Aircraft, North American Aviation, Sperry Corporation and United Aircraft and Transport, for an account that he was managing.

He chose these specific companies because he thought that they were the leading companies in this area. He was particularly impressed by their strong balance sheets (which he felt would allow them to withstand any problems), valuable patents (which gave them an advantage over their competitors), and the depth of their experience. Five years later, (adjusting for the fact that United Aircraft and Transport was broken up into separate companies), the share prices of the quintet had risen by an average of 332% (325% if you weigh the increase according to the number of shares that Price purchased in each company). In contrast, the value of the Dow Jones only went up by 53% during the same period, while stocks in the mature railroad sector declined.

Another stock that proved to be extremely lucrative for Price was IBM, one of the first companies that his Growth Fund invested in after it was set up in 1950. He would continue to hold IBM stock in his portfolio through to his retirement, which meant that the fund benefited from IBM's domination of the rapidly growing mainframe market in the 1950s and 60s. However, after his retirement the Growth Fund would arguably become too attached to the computer company, continuing to hold it as it ran into problems during the 1980s.

Other lessons for investors

As well as giving advice about which companies to buy, Price had plenty to say about how you should buy (and sell). Instead of buying a load of shares in a company all at once, he split his stock purchases over a gradual period, only stopping when the stock had become too expensive or if something happened that convinced him it was no longer an attractive acquisition. This allowed him to monitor how a company was doing before committing all of his capital. It also reduced the impact of short-term price fluctuations.

Price would also get out of a position in a similar way. After a company had risen 30% above the maximum level that he was willing to pay for a share, Price would sell a chunk of the company. The remaining shares would also be gradually sold after each further 10% rise in value. This allowed him to benefit from any further appreciation, something that wouldn't have happened had he sold immediately, while resisting the temptation to hold on to a company long after it became too expensive.

Overall, Price teaches investors that it is important to strike a balance between consistency and flexibility. While chopping and changing your strategy is clearly no way to succeed (not least because it leads to huge trading costs), even the best strategy has to take into account a change in circumstances (in Price's case, sky-high valuations at the end of the 1960s). While professional investors may be boxed in by their past reputation and the demands of clients and employers, those managing their own accounts face far fewer constraints.

RATING
T. ROWE PRICE

Performance: *T. Rowe Price's public fund only narrowly beat the market, though this was good enough to turn his company into a large operation. However, his accounts for private clients did much better.*
(★★★★)

Longevity: *Price was involved in the market for over 40 years.*
(★★★★★)

Influence: *Along with Philip Fisher, Price played a significant role in developing growth investing as a major strategy.* (★★★★)

Ease of replication: *T. Rowe Price's more pragmatic approach to growth investing needs a little bit more work than Fisher's, because it involves more frequent buying and selling. Investors who want to follow Price will have to take into account the conditions of an overall industry as well as how expensive a company is.* (★★★)

Overall rating: 16 out of 20

CHAPTER 11

Peter Lynch

===

The Man Who Beat the Street

Introduction

P HILIP FISHER AND T. Rowe Price both did a lot to lay the early
ground rules for growth investing. However, Peter Lynch gave it a
new twist. As a fund manager he earned huge returns over a 13-year period,
turning a relatively small mutual fund into a behemoth. As the author of
two very successful books on investing, he encouraged millions of people to
invest money in the stock market directly. Indeed, his idea that individual
investors can beat the professionals, and that you should "buy what you
know", has been credited with leading to the surge of public interest in
investing that took place during the 1990s.

Of course, while it's great to be the public face of Wall Street when stock
prices are rising, it's not such a good thing on the way down. After the bull
market reached its peak in the technology-fuelled bubble of 1999–2000,
and then imploded, Lynch received a lot of blame, even though he had
long since retired. Indeed, in recent interviews he has repeatedly tried to
disassociate himself from the more extreme and simplistic versions of his
message. Despite this, he is undeniably an investing legend, and one who
has a lot of lessons for the average investor, even if his investing style was
actually more complicated than it appeared.

From the golf course to fund management

Born in 1944, Peter Lynch grew up near Boston. He became interested in investing as a result of getting a job as a caddy at a golf club and overhearing clients discuss various companies. Indeed, one of the stock tips that he heard on the golf course – the cargo airline Flying Tiger Line – would prove so lucrative that it would go a long way to paying both the cost of his university studies at Boston College and his graduate studies at Wharton. (Ironically, a large chunk of the cost of his initial degree was already paid for by a golf scholarship.)

Caddying for George Sullivan, the president of the mutual fund company Fidelity, also put Lynch in a prime position to get a coveted internship with Fidelity in 1966. This summer job also meant that after Wharton and a brief stint in the US Army, he was hired as an analyst in 1969. Despite Lynch's initial lucky breaks, he then worked his way up through the ranks, becoming Fidelity's director of research in 1974. By 1979 he was put in charge of the relatively small Magellan mutual fund.

Over the next 13 years, Lynch would run Magellan until his retirement in 1990. At the same time, he would also manage a pension fund for several large companies, including Kodak, Ford and Eaton. After stepping down from directly managing money, Lynch would continue to give advice to Fidelity as well as become a respected financial commentator. Lynch would also write a series of investment books, including *One Up on Wall Street* (first published in 1989), *Beating the Street* (first published in 1993) and *Learn to Earn* (1995).

Bottom-up investing

In his book *One Up on Wall Street*, Peter Lynch divided the stock market into six groups: mature slow-growing companies, stalwart blue-chips, cyclical stocks which followed the economy, fast-growers, turnarounds, and companies with hidden assets. Of these six groups, he would avoid slow-growing companies, since they had exhausted their potential. He would buy a few blue-chips if he felt that they still had longer to run, and get involved the occasional asset play if the opportunity was attractive enough. However, most of his portfolio was devoted to two strategies: 'thematic' plays on industries that he felt were doing better than the market expected and bets on individual companies.

When dealing with entire industries, Lynch would tend to buy a wide range of related companies. Although this meant that his portfolio frequently contained large numbers of individual stocks, the fact that they were all in similar lines of business meant that the portfolio was still actively invested, rather than behaving like a closet index fund which just followed the overall market. Splitting his bets between similar companies also allowed him to invest an increasingly large amount of money without falling foul of regulations that limited the percentage of his portfolio he could put into each individual company (as well as the percentage of each individual company he could own).

The other half of Lynch's portfolio, and the area that he was most interested in, was bottom-up investing in companies that he felt were particularly well run, irrespective of the industry in which they were in. Indeed, if the fundamentals of the individual companies were strong enough, he was happy to put money into industries that were slower-growing, stagnant or even in a few cases were declining. He cautioned that investors who just looked at 'hot' sectors, without looking at the quality of individual firms, risked being disappointed. Not only did they suffer from unrealistic expectations, they were vulnerable to being overtaken by competitors.

Ideally, Lynch liked his bottom-up investments to have a reasonable balance sheet, with not too much debt, and a price/earnings ratio that was equal to their growth rate. However, he believed that spending too much time on company finances or valuation could be counterproductive. Firstly, he believed that an expensive but fast-growing company would always do better than one which was cheaper but expanding more slowly. Similarly, and more importantly, even the best financial ratios were backward-looking, telling the investor about what had happened in the past but providing little insight about the future.

As a result, Lynch focused more on trying to evaluate a company's "story", his term for the skills of the management and the quality of the products the firm was selling. Part of this came via the traditional fund manager route of directly speaking to management, both about their own companies, but also which competitors they were most afraid of. However, unlike most of his fund manager rivals, Lynch also liked to do more practical research. For firms that directly sold to the public, this involved visiting their premises and even trying out products himself (or getting his friends and family to do so).

Outpacing the bull

Lynch was lucky to have operated during a time when the stock market was booming, with the S&P 500 rising from 96 at the end of May 1977 to 361 exactly 13 years later. Despite this, his performance was even more exceptional, as $1,000 invested in the Magellan Fund when Lynch took over in 1977 would have been $28,000 when he retired 13 years later – an annualised return of just less than 30%. It should come as no surprise that investors rushed to have their money invested with him, with the fund's assets under management rising from $18m to $12bn.

Magellan's returns were higher at the start, so investors who piled into the fund in later years didn't do quite as well. However, overall it was consistently successful, managing to beat the stock market in 11 out of its 13 years. Perhaps the biggest compliment that Lynch received was that his departure from Magellan led not to praise but anger – from investors who had made a lot of money and wanted him to stay on so that he could make them even more. Lynch didn't give any public numbers for the pension money that he managed, but would claim his returns were even better than his mutual fund during the same period (he also stepped down from the pension groups at the same time).

Liked the company, bought its shares, made a packet

Two examples that illustrate both parts of Lynch's approach to investing are the car company Chrysler and clothing firm Hanes Corporation. During the early 1980s, the US economy was in a deep recession, leading to plunging car sales. Lynch believed that eventually Americans would have to start buying cars again, which would boost the entire sector. After talking to senior executives from Ford Motor Company, he got the impression that Chrysler, seen as on the verge of bankruptcy, was in the best position to benefit from any rebound.

This was confirmed by a visit to Chrysler itself, where he was impressed by the quality of the new cars that they were developing (especially their new minivan). He also thought that their new CEO, Lee Iacocca, was able to turn the company around. A scrutiny of its balance sheet also revealed that the car company was about to get a large sum of cash from the sale of its military division, enabling the company to survive in the short and medium term. As a result, Lynch aggressively bought shares in Chrysler up to the 5% maximum permitted by the rules, while he also put money in other car companies like Ford and Volvo.

This bet on the car sector worked well, with the entire industry rebounding. However, his decision to focus mainly on Chrysler was an even bigger success. Indeed, it surged from $2, when he started buying in bulk, to a peak of around $50 a share just before the October 1987 mini-crash. While Lynch ended up holding the company a bit too long, it was still around $25 when he finally sold out in 1988 – a 1,150% price return in only six years.

If Chrysler was an example of how product research can supplement more traditional analysis, Hanes Corporation is a successful example of the reverse: Lynch initially found out about the firm after his wife commentated favourably on L'eggs, a brand of tights that Hanes was trialling in stores. Of course, before he decided to buy he then did further research. This showed that L'eggs already accounted for a significant portion of Hanes's sales, so that its success would have a large impact on the bottom line. It also revealed that Hanes was the only major company to sell branded tights in convenience stores, making them much more accessible.

Similarly, when a competitor came out with a rival product that threatened to steal market share from Hanes, he asked her to test the competitor's offering. When she reported that the new product was inferior, and was therefore unlikely to displace L'eggs, Lynch was reassured enough to hold on to the share. He ended up being amply rewarded. Indeed, by the time Hanes was taken over by Sara Lee, its share price had gone up by six times.

Growth investing simplified

It's hard for the average investor to replicate Peter Lynch's access to company management, the team of analysts he had under him at Fidelity, or his remarkable energy, which saw him working seven days a week. Indeed, it turned out that even Lynch couldn't maintain his workaholic habits, blaming his relatively early retirement on the demands of his job. However, Lynch believed that the average investor could compensate for this by her knowledge of a particular industry, either because she worked in it or was just a keen customer.

Indeed, he would argue that in some cases you actually have an advantage over Wall Street professionals, who tended to ignore such intelligence. Of course, Lynch would emphasise that this knowledge was only part of the puzzle. Indeed, in a recent interview he said, "I've never said, 'If you go to a mall, see a Starbucks and say it's good coffee, you should call Fidelity brokerage and buy the stock'." He felt that even the most informed customer would always be less-informed than someone who had a much more meaningful relationship with it. However, combined with a rudimentary understanding of financial ratios, and the product or brand's importance to the actual share, it should be possible to sniff out some opportunities.

RATING
PETER LYNCH

Performance: *Fidelity's Magellan Fund beat the market by a very large amount during Lynch's tenure as portfolio manager.* (★★★★★)

Longevity: *Peter Lynch's tenure at Fidelity lasted just over a decade, although he did invest his own money before then.* (★★★)

Influence: *Peter Lynch popularised the idea of 'buying what you know' and has been credited (and blamed) for encouraging a generation of retail investors to get into the stock market.* (★★★★)

Ease of replication: *Peter Lynch's strategy of meeting with the management of hundreds of companies proved impractical for him, as shown by his early retirement, let alone ordinary investors. However, his idea of using your own day-to-day experiences of a company to guide your investing is a useful tip for ordinary investors, provided it isn't taken too literally.* (★★★)

Overall rating: 15 out of 20

CHAPTER 12
Nick Train

═══

The Inactive Optimist

Introduction

A LL FUND MANAGERS like to say that they believe in buying shares and holding them for the long term. In reality, few of them actually do so. In fact, they seem to be taking a much more short-term perspective than they used to. According to data by LPL Financial, as late as the 1960s, the average holding period of a share listed on the New York Stock Exchange was as long as eight years. Today it is around five days. Of course, this figure is distorted by day traders, as well as high-frequency traders who buy and sell large amounts of shares in a fraction of a second. However, SCM Miller calculates that the average UK fund turns over nearly 90% of its portfolio each year.

Not only does this incur large trading costs, there is little evidence that it does anything to boost returns. Ironically, this hyperactive approach to trading does little to hide the fact that a large proportion of fund managers are 'closet indexers', spreading their investment between a large number of familiar names, with little apparent enthusiasm for any individual company. One noted investor who takes a completely different approach, slothful when it comes to trading but at the same time very active, is the growth investor Nick Train.

Apprentice becomes
the master

Nick Train graduated from Oxford with a degree in modern history in 1981. Despite seriously considering an academic career, he decided instead to join investment firm GT Management. Early on in his career he would read *The Money Masters* (1980) by his namesake John Train, a book profiling various successful investors, which he credits with shaping his investment philosophy. For over a decade he would manage GT's income fund, rising to the position of chief investment officer for pan-Europe. However, when GT was taken over by Invesco, Train decided to move to M&G as director of investment management.

Shortly after joining M&G, Nick Train was quickly promoted to head of global equities. However, after only two years he decided to leave in order to set up his own investment firm, Lindsell Train, with Mike Lindsell, who had also worked for GT Management. Since December 2000, Train has run the Finsbury Growth and Income Investment Trust. At the same time he also runs two other funds: the Lindsell Train Investment Trust (since January 2001) and CF Lindsell Train UK Equity (since July 2006), while he also co-manages Lindsell Train Global Equity.

Finding value in growth

On the surface, Nick Train is a rather unconventional growth investor. Indeed, he prefers to call himself a value investor, agreeing with Benjamin Graham that shares have a definite intrinsic value and that you shouldn't own a share unless you believe it to be undervalued. What's more, he also cites Warren Buffett as a key influence. However, while Buffett has evolved from buying good companies at bargain prices to investing in great companies at good prices, Train is willing to pay almost any price for exceptional companies. Indeed he believes, from his own internal research, that truly great companies are worth up to 60 times their current earnings.

Another thing that puts him squarely in the growth camp is his extreme reluctance to sell a company that is doing well. While value investors tend to dump shares that have increased in price so much that they no longer look 'cheap', Train thinks that you should stick with them. Indeed, he has criticised money managers for what he sees as their readiness to take profits by selling shares that have made them money. The only time Train will sell a share is if he thinks that its long-term growth prospects have significantly worsened, arguing that there are so few great companies that once you've found one you should hold on to it.

Train's reluctance to sell successful investments means that he has a low turnover of around 5% a year, which means on average he should turnover his entire portfolio once every two decades. Indeed, there have been several years when he hasn't moved any companies either in or out of his portfolio. This is an extraordinarily low level, given that many of his competitors change their entire portfolio every year, and helps to keep his transaction costs very low.

Another key difference between him and other managers is that he doesn't believe in excessive diversification, with the top ten investments in Finsbury Growth and Income accounting for 68% of assets. Lindsell Train UK Equity is even more concentrated, with 83.9% of the fund in just ten companies. Overall, his approach can be summed up as the idea that, if you hold on to a handful of very strong companies, and you hold them over time, you will automatically do well.

Buying shares in good-tasting companies

Train has several rules of thumb for finding those few exceptional companies that are worthy of a place in his portfolio. Like Peter Lynch, he thinks that good product quality and lots of customer appreciation are big indications of potential growth. As well as enabling a company to build sales, selling a product that tastes good, or that consumers really love, helps insulate a company from the economic cycle and generates a healthy cash flow. Train also believes that a strong brand will help defend against the threats of competition and technological change, making it easier for investors to be certain that revenue growth will continue well into the future.

Train likes companies that are controlled by a single family, or where a family at least has a big stake. In his view, family ownership provides a discipline that encourages firms to allocate capital efficiently. They are also more likely to take a long-term view, looking at the challenges and opportunities over the next 10 to 20 years, rather than just the next couple of quarters. In contrast, most professional managers have little stake in a firm's success and are in any case likely to stay in one place for only a limited period. Having operations around the world, rather than in just one country, can also help boost profitability.

Finally, Train thinks it vital that investors know and understand what they are investing in. No matter how big a company's potential, he will stay away if it has an overly complex business model or if he doesn't really understand what it does. For example, while he thinks that the biotechnology sector could do well in the next few years, he has joked that he should be sacked if he ever considers buying the shares of a biotech company because he knows little about the science underpinning the industry. This doesn't mean that he is completely adverse to technology companies, just that he wants them to have a simple business model. In an example of 'buy what you know', Train put money into software firm Sage after being impressed with their accounting software, which his office uses (Train describes himself as "innumerate").

Stocks – and stock markets – for the long run

Train also considers himself an economic optimist, and sees this optimism as a core part of his investment strategy. While he thinks that attempting to invest on the basis of short-term economic forecasts is a fool's errand, he believes that the medium and long-term outlook is very rosy. Despite short-term price increases, he thinks that input costs are generally declining. Indeed, he notes that commodity and energy prices have been falling relative to finished goods and services for over three centuries.

He also thinks that digital technology and improvements in business organisation are set to deliver major productivity gains and reduce the amount of working capital that firms will need. This will in turn allow them to return more money to shareholders. Finally, he thinks that there is a lot of scope for both industry consolidation, which will boost margins and eliminate waste, and cross-border mergers, improving efficiency and spreading best practice throughout the world.

Of course, if profits do increase then it's logical that the share prices of the underlying companies should also follow suit. So, it's unsurprising that Train's economic optimism naturally leads him to be very bullish about stock returns. This is reinforced by the fact that, as Train himself has pointed out, over extended periods, shares have produced very strong returns, outperforming both bonds and cash. Of course, if shares do well, then industries that depend on the stock market should also benefit. So he believes that it makes sense to invest in infrastructure like the exchanges themselves. He also thinks that the fund management industry should also benefit from strong stock market performance.

Exceptional performance

From the start of January 2001 to the end of March 2017, £100 invested in the Finsbury Growth and Income Investment Trust would have grown to be worth £560 (including reinvested dividends), an annual return of just over 11%. The Lindsell Train Investment Trust has done even better, with £100 invested at its March 2001 inception turning into £878.90 some 16 years later, equivalent to 14.54% a year. Around two-fifths of the latter fund is invested in

Lindsell Train itself (which is not listed). Both these funds have outperformed the FTSE All-Share, which has returned only 121% (5% a year), including dividends, during this period. Between 2007 and 2016, Lindsell Train Global Equity rose by 194.3% (12.73%), compared with 74.3% for the FTSE (6.35%).

As a result of his success, the Lindsell Train Investment Trust now trades at a whopping premium of 30% to the value of its net asset value. In other words, investors value Nick Train's management skills so highly that they are willing to pay a 30% premium to the value of the shares in his portfolio (which at one point reached 70%), even thought most investment trusts trade at a discount to the value of the portfolio. Indeed, Train has warned investors that he considers the premium to be excessive. Meanwhile the open-ended Lindsell Train Global Equity Fund now has £3.4bn of assets under management.

What has worked...

Nick Train's most successful investment was in the football club Manchester United, when he was still at GT Management. He bought the club during the early 90s (the club was floated in 1991). He felt that its name recognition and international supporter base would ensure that it would benefit hugely from the explosion in revenue from television money. During the 1990s, this prediction was proven correct as the amount paid by television companies increased from £60m to £170m a season by the end of the 90s, thanks to the development of the Premier League. As a result, Train saw the value of his investment soar – the shares increased by over 30 times.

Another investment that has been extremely profitable has been in the clothing firm Burberry. In this case, Train kept track of it for a number of years before deciding to buy. While he greatly admired the quality of its products, he thought that it was too expensive, even for him. However, when it halved in price during the height of the financial crisis to £3.60, he started buying it, and then bought even more when it continued to fall to £1.60.

While Burberry quickly bounced back to over £5.65 a share within a year, Train decided to hold on to it because he admired the quality of its clothes and branded goods. Shares are now £17.85, an increase of around 20% a year from his initial buying price (and 30% a year from its bottom). While it trades at over 30× trailing earnings, an amount that other fund managers would consider very high, Train still thinks that it has a lot of potential because he admires the firm's success in making money from online sales and the quality of its digital marketing.

...and what hasn't

Not all of Train's investments have worked out. One of his few missteps has been his investment in the educational publisher Pearson. The company has seen both its margins and sales hit by the shift from physical textbooks to online books and learning materials. This has had a knock-on effect on its share price, which is substantially lower than it was 15 years ago. While Train has decided to stick with his investment, he has admitted that he has come close to selling it on several occasions, and even apologised to investors for the negative effect that its performance has had on his portfolios.

Another company that wasn't able to deal with the change in technology was EMI, one of his earliest purchases for the Finsbury investment trust. Train admits that he didn't grasp the extent to which technology, especially online piracy and file-sharing and the replacement of high-margin CDs by downloads, would destroy both revenue and profitability. However, once he realised his mistake he got out of it quickly, selling all his shares in 2003.

Keeping it simple

Nick Train proves that it is possible to beat the market over several economic cycles without a lot of feverish buying and selling. Indeed, his idea of buying quality companies, with simple businesses, and holding on to them, is a strategy that should be particularly attractive to investors who have a limited amount of time. It also shows that value investing isn't the only way to make money in the stock market. Still, his approach isn't without its potential problems. His experience with Pearson shows the downside of 'falling in love' with a company, especially since even quality companies can end up being crippled by technological change or a smart competitor.

RATING
NICK TRAIN

Performance: *The funds and trusts that Nick Train has run under the Lindsell Train umbrella have substantially outperformed the market.* (★★★★)

Longevity: *Nick Train has been involved with Lindsell Train for nearly two decades. Before then he was a fund manager for various other companies.* (★★★★)

Influence: *While Nick Train has been an extremely successful investor he has deliberately kept an extremely low profile.* (★)

Ease of replication: *Buying a small group of shares in high-quality growth companies that can deliver consistent returns and holding them for long periods is one of the least stressful ways to make money in the stock market. It is also the approach that is most accessible to ordinary investors who have a limited amount of time. However, the trick is to identify the small number of exceptional companies that can actually do this.* (★★★★)

Overall rating: 13 out of 20

CHAPTER 13

Georges Doriot

===

The Venture Capital Pioneer

Introduction

VENTURE CAPITAL IS now a major part of global capital markets. Indeed, Ernst & Young estimated that in 2015 alone venture capital firms invested $148bn in 8,381 deals, mostly in the US, Europe and China. Virtually all listed technology companies have taken venture capital funding at some point. However, while there have always been informal groups of private investors, it was not until the end of the second world war that 'seed investing' became formalised. While other individuals, such as John Hay Whitney and William Draper, also played an important role, the acknowledged pioneer was Georges Doriot.

Given that venture capital is so strongly associated with the United States, and that European policymakers have bemoaned the fact that Europe apparently lags behind in this regard, it is ironic that the person who is credited with inventing the industry was an immigrant from France. Born in Paris in 1899, Georges Doriot briefly dropped out of university to serve as an officer in an artillery unit during the first world war. However, after the war ended and he had finished his studies, he realised that his opportunities in a country devastated by war were very limited.

As a result, Doriot emigrated to the US, with the plan of studying at MIT. However, an encounter with the Dean of Harvard Business School persuaded him to study at Harvard Business School for a year instead. He then worked at the Wall Street firm Kuhn, Loeb & Co. for four years. In 1925 he returned to Harvard Business School, becoming a full professor by

1929. Indeed, even as a postwar venture capitalist, he would continue to teach courses at HBS, and by the time he retired from lecturing in 1966, he had taught around 7,000 students.

As well as carrying out a great deal of informal consulting, Doriot also taught at the US Army Industrial College during the 1930s. As America moved towards a war footing, a former pupil persuaded him to serve in the US Army as a quartermaster, giving him a big influence over the direction of war production and military technology. By the end of the second world war, Doriot had risen to the rank of brigadier general (a title that he continued to use in civilian life). This job also put him in close contact with a large number of leading manufacturers and researchers.

Doriot's experience meant that he was approached by industrialist (later US senator) Ralph Flanders to become the CEO of American Research and Development Corporation (ARDC), a professional venture capital fund set up in 1946. Doriot would run ARDC for a quarter century until his retirement in 1971 (a year later ARDC would be merged with the technology conglomerate Textron). He would also play a key role in setting up two other venture capital funds: the Canadian Enterprise Development Corporation (CED) and the European Enterprise Development Company (EED).

Buying a stake in a business

ARDC was founded on the principle that the huge expansion in government funding for science, and the large pool of skilled labour created by the GI Bill, would create a large number of business opportunities, especially for returning servicemen. The idea was that ARDC would supply enough capital to these fledgling businesses to enable them to become big enough to be floated on the stock market. In return ARDC would receive a large equity stake in the companies. The founders believed that the process of funding small start-up companies would help America to maintain its technological edge and diversify away from maturing industries like steel and heavy manufacturing, though the primary objective was obviously to make money.

Another part of Doriot's strategy was an insistence on sticking with investments for extended periods, rather than selling at the first opportunity, even if his companies initially produced little or no return. In many cases ARDC even retained a substantial stake after a company was floated on the stock market (the natural exit point for many VCs even today). While many on Wall Street saw such attitudes as overly sentimental, Doriot argued that his experience as a professor and a consultant had taught him that time and patience were required for a company to realise its long-term potential. As a result, he argued that a patient approach would produce higher rewards when the companies were eventually sold or floated in the stock market.

Another way in which ARDC differed from its predecessors was its discriminating attitude to selecting investments. Before it arrived on the scene, family foundations or individuals had provided what little venture capital there was, and they relied on social or business contacts, haphazardly putting money into companies run by their friends. Doriot believed in judging each request for venture capital on its merits, and only putting money behind the very best ideas.

A keen researcher, Doriot and his staff would do a huge amount of due diligence to select the best ideas from the hundreds of proposals that reached them, as well as the many interesting ideas that they had heard about. This due diligence focused on two areas: the quality of the business plan and the entrepreneurial skills of the leadership.

Short-term problems, long-term success

Initially the idea of venture capital investing met with a huge degree of scepticism from Wall Street. The large foundations viewed it as too risky, while many financiers believed that Doriot was more interested in building up companies than turning a profit. As a result, ARDC's initial public offering in 1946 only managed to raise $3.5m ($42.5m at 2015 prices), rather than the $5m ($60.6m) that it was aiming for.

During the first decade the company's performance was poor. Between 1946 and 1957, ARDC's per-share value of its assets grew by only 37.8%, a mediocre annual return of 3.3%. Even this may be a generous measure, since there was no way to properly measure the value of companies that had neither made profits nor paid dividends. Indeed, the actual price of ARDC's shares traded below their initial level of $25, which meant that investors who needed to cash out would have lost money. At one point shares in the fund could be bought for only $16, a fall of a third.

Indeed, initial poor performance would lead to MIT deciding to sell all its stake in Doriot's fund. What made this particularly galling was the fact that the trustee in charge of the investment was also the treasurer of ARDC, suggesting that even the company's executives had no confidence in the way it was run. At the same time key staff resigned, feeling that the structure of the company meant that they were poorly paid considering the effort that they put in (most subsequent venture capital funds would be run as limited partnerships).

However, ARDC's shares would take off in the late 1950s and 60s. Indeed, prices would rise so much that it underwent a three-for-one stock split in 1960 and a four-for-one split in 1969. A secondary offering in 1960 would also raise an additional $8m ($64m). Overall, the firm had net assets of $427m ($2.5bn) by the time Doriot retired in 1971. Adjusting for the stock splits and the infusion of capital, net assets per share would rise just under 35 times over 25 years, a return of over 15% a year, much higher than the overall stock market.

Sadly, not all of Doriot's other schemes were as successful as ARDC. Indeed, the European Enterprise Development Company (EED) failed in 1976 (after being founded in 1963). Doriot would blame this on the fact that it was run by bankers who had little patience for technology investing, and that the business environment was hostile to start-up investing. The Canadian Enterprise Development Corporation (CED) would also be dissolved in 1986.

Doriot's best investment –
Digital Electronic Corporation

Doriot (and ARDC's) most famous investment was in Digital Electronic Corporation. DEC was founded by two MIT researchers, Ken Olsen and Harlan Anderson. Their idea was to build smaller computers (minicomputers) that could be used by other researchers and scientists, in contrast to the huge room-sized mainframes that were used by large companies. Although the duo's prototype TX-O was a big hit with the students at MIT (even though faster computers were available), companies were extremely reluctant to give them the capital support that they required to start out in business, because even established companies (such as RCA) had failed to break into the market.

After listening to a presentation from the duo, Doriot decided to invest $70,000 ($589,000 in 2015 prices) in DEC in return for 70% of the equity in the company. He also gave the founders plenty of advice (though he didn't interfere in day-to-day decisions). This proved to be a very good decision, as DEC moved into profit in a very short space of time, thanks to the success of the PDP-1 computer. By 1966, DEC was in a strong enough position to be able go public. A year after that, ARDC's stake in the company was worth $125m, accounting for 80% of the value of its 45-company portfolio. At its peak in the late 1980s, DEC had revenues of $14bn, and would be bought in 1998 by Compaq for $9.6bn.

Lessons from ARDC

Despite the emergence of equity crowdfunding in recent years, few retail investors are in a position to directly invest in a company. However, Doriot's experience with ARDC can teach us several things about investing in small-cap and early-stage technology companies. Just as ARDC was undervalued by the market in its first decade, it can take time for the market to properly value companies that have few tangible sales or profits (though this can mean that companies can be overvalued as well as undervalued). As a result, proper technology investing requires the patience to stick with a company, even though its stock price is lagging the market.

Like venture capital, technology investing is also about finding a couple of star performers that will compensate for the large number of companies that either do poorly or fail altogether. The most obvious illustration of this comes from ARDC itself. Indeed, had Doriot passed on DEC, his fund's annual returns would have been a much more modest 7.4% over 25 years of operation, well below the performance of the market during this period. As a result, diversification is even more important than with normal investing. However, you still should avoid over-diversification, as it will prevent you from electively focusing on the most profitable opportunities.

It is also important to do your own research, rather than relying on either the promotional material provided by a firm or the opinions of others. After all, few business owners will admit that there are flaws in something that they have invested a huge amount of time and energy setting up. Similarly, people can be too eager to write off a new technology, simply because another firm failed to fully exploit it. Just as initial failures to develop minicomputers meant that people were reluctant to invest in DEC, the excesses of the internet bubble of 1999–2000 hid the fact that in many cases the ideas were good, just a little ahead of their time.

Indeed, in many cases a visionary leader at the helm of a company can make the difference between success and failure. As a result, investors should follow Doriot's example of paying attention to the quality of a company's management when deciding whether to invest.

RATING
GEORGES DORIOT

Performance: *ARDC comfortably outperformed the market over its 25 years of operation. However, the failure of Doriot's other venture capital funds blot his record somewhat.* (★★★★)

Longevity: *Doriot would be involved with ARDC for 25 years.* (★★★★)

Influence: *As the founder of the first venture capital fund, Doriot is rightly credited with creating the venture capital industry.* (★★★★★)

Ease of replication: *Directly investing in venture capital is generally not possible for investors unless you have a large amount of capital to deploy, though there are some listed funds and there are plenty of small-cap technology companies listed on the stock market.* (★★)

Overall rating: 15 out of 20

He chose these specific companies because he thought that they were the leading companies in this area. He was particularly impressed by their strong balance sheets (which he felt would allow them to withstand any problems), valuable patents (which gave them an advantage over their competitors), and the depth of their experience. Five years later, (adjusting for the fact that United Aircraft and Transport was broken up into separate companies), the share prices of the quintet had risen by an average of 512% (325% if you weigh the increase according to the number of shares that Price purchased in each company). In contrast, the value of the Dow Jones only went up by 15% during the same period, while stocks in the mature railroad sector declined.

Another stock that proved to be extremely lucrative for Price was IBM, one of the first companies that his Growth Fund invested in after it was set up in 1950. He would continue to hold IBM stock in his portfolio through to his retirement, which meant that the fund benefited from IBM's domination of the rapidly growing mainframe market in the 1950s and 60s. However, after his retirement the Growth Fund would arguably become too attached to the computer company, continuing to hold it as it ran into problems during the 1980s.

Other Lessons for Investors

As well as giving advice about which companies to buy, Price had plenty to say about how you should buy (and sell). Instead of buying a load of shares in a company all at once, he split his stock purchases over a gradual period, only stopping when the stock had become too expensive or if something happened that convinced him it was no longer an attractive acquisition. This allowed him to monitor how a company was doing before committing all of his capital. It also reduced the impact of short-term price fluctuations.

Price would also get out of a position in a similar way. After a company had risen 30% above the maximum level that he was willing to pay for a

CHAPTER 14
Eugene Kleiner &
Tom Perkins

≡

The VCs of Silicon Valley

Introduction

GEORGES DORIOT MAY have put the venture capital industry on a more formal footing by creating the first venture-capital fund that the general public could invest in. However, it was not until the 1970s that venture capital began to take off and emerge as a serious asset class. The main reason for this was the rise of the computer and biotechnology industries in Northern California (the area that would later become known as Silicon Valley). These two industry sectors were expanding at a breakneck pace and needed seed capital, but were too risky for more conventional sources of funding such as bank loans or public offerings.

In contrast, the venture-capital industry was a much better partner for Silicon Valley as it was willing to make a lot of losing investments in order for one or two to strike it rich. The development of the venture capital industry was further boosted in the late 1970s by changes to securities law, which made it much easier for pension funds, endowments and other trusts to put money into the investment groups created by venture capitalists. Paul Gompers of Harvard Business School estimates that, in the two decades from 1972, venture capitalists would bring 962 companies to the point where they could be listed on the stock exchange.

While many people made huge fortunes during this period, no firm would be more influential in both setting the rules of the game and funnelling capital to various companies than Kleiner Perkins (now Kleiner Perkins Caufield & Byers). While KPCB is no longer the industry leader, it was wildly successful in its first 15 years, and provided the template that many of its competitors still follow. Kleiner Perkins was founded and developed in 1972 by investors Eugene Kleiner and Tom Perkins (the other two partners, Frank Caulfield and Brook Byers, would not join until 1977).

The refugee and the executive

Born in Austria in 1923, Eugene Kleiner's father fled his home country shortly after the German invasion in 1938. After brief periods in Brussels, Spain and finally Portugal, the Kleiner family found itself on a ship for New York. Kleiner would briefly train as a machinist before being called into the US Army, where his German language skills meant that he would spend the second world war guarding a prisoner of war camp. After leaving the army he did an engineering degree at Brooklyn Polytechnic College (now part of NYU), followed by a master's at New York University.

After working as an engineer for Western Electric, Kleiner made the fateful decision to take a job with Nobel Prize winner William Shockley. Not only did this mean that he moved to California, but it also put him in contact with a team of extremely talented scientists. Unfortunately (or fortunately as it turned out) Shockley was such a bad manager that he managed to quickly alienate the entire staff. Indeed, things got so bad that the team struck out on their own, with Kleiner using his contacts to persuade a rival company to invest in them.

The resulting company, Fairchild Semiconductor, was such a success that the owner exercised his option to buy the team out after only three years, earning each member of the team $250,000 ($2m at 2015 prices.) While this was a tiny sum compared to the importance of the technology, it would provide Kleiner with enough capital to become an investor. For the next 12 years Kleiner continued to be involved in technology firms, founding his own company Edex, sold to Raytheon in 1965 for $5m. He would also invest in other early-stage technology companies, most notably Intel, founded by former colleagues Gordon Moore and Robert Noyce.

In contrast to Kleiner, Tom Perkins's background was much more conventional. Born in White Plains, New York in 1932, he studied engineering at MIT, where he came into contact with Georges Doriot, and did an MBA at Harvard. He then took a marketing job at Hewlett-Packard, then a small but fast-growing technology company. While he would leave HP for a while to work for an unsuccessful start-up, he would return and keep ascending the corporate ladder. Indeed, he was responsible for not only turning the computer division from a sideshow into the core of the firm, but also restructuring it in order to deal with its greatly increased size.

However, the owners of HP made it clear to him that he was never going to become the CEO. At the same time he had invested in a start-up, University Laboratories, which was eventually bought out by Spectra-Physics, earning him millions. Newly rich, and wanting to move on to other challenges, Perkins believed that there was an urgent need in the technology sector for early-stage funding that was not being met by either the traditional institutions or the few venture capital firms that existed. As a result, he left HP to set up his own venture capital firm. While trying to raise money, an investment banker suggested that he partner with Kleiner, who was trying to do the same thing.

Kleiner Perkins was therefore founded in 1972 and would begin making investments in companies a year later. By 1986 Eugene Kleiner would formally step down from day-to-day involvement in KP's business, though he would stay on as an informal advisor. Similarly, Perkins would also eventually step aside, though he would maintain a relationship with KP and the companies that it helped fund. Investments that Perkins was involved with included Amazon, Netscape and Google. While Perkins never disclosed his actual fortune, denying reports that it was more than $1bn, he had enough money to spend over $150m on a yacht.

Investing in edible dog food

Before Kleiner Perkins was founded, it was normal for venture capitalists to be passive investors. This meant that while they paid a lot of attention to selecting good companies to invest in, they didn't directly intervene in either day-to-day management or strategic decisions of those companies. However, Tom Perkins and Eugene Kleiner's previous experience meant that they were both convinced that a more direct approach was necessary. As a result, KP took an active role in determining how the companies that it invested in were run. This included taking seats on boards of directors and even bringing in outside executives to help a founder run the company.

Another important factor in determining whether they invested in a particular project was whether there was going to be a market for the technology around which the company was based. While this may sound obvious, they both knew that scientists could get sidetracked by the elegance of a technology, without considering whether it could make money. As Kleiner would famously say, "after R&D is finished, make sure that the dogs want to eat the dog food". He also disliked the idea of focusing on tiny markets, arguing that "new companies dividing niche markets are like two bald men fighting over a comb".

Two big successes

One of KP's most famous successes was investing in the biotechnology pioneer Genentech. Genentech was founded in 1976 by Herbert Boyer, a professor at the University of California San Francisco, and Robert Swanson, who had worked for Cetus Technologies, a company that Kleiner Perkins had invested in. The idea was to use the new technology of genetic engineering to produce human insulin and other medical therapies. After discussing things with KP, and checking the technology with outside consultants, they agreed to invest $100,000 (later increased to $200,000), provided Tom Perkins was appointed chairman of the new company.

Instead of directly trying to produce insulin, which would have required a huge amount of money, Genentech focused on the much simpler task of producing the hormone somatostatin, which they did successfully. While it had only limited commercial value, it proved that the technology was viable. As a result, Genentech was able to agree a partnership with a drug company to produce human insulin. Under this deal the drug company paid a lot of the costs of the research. By 1978 this goal was achieved, making headlines around the world.

Two years later, the company would be listed on the stock market, with KP's 938,800 shares worth $35 each for a total of $32.5m. This was a return of over 162× in less than four years. By 1986, a decade on from KP's investment, the value of its stake had increased to $160m, which meant that its value effectively doubled each year. Overall, according to data provided by Christopher Golis, the value of Kleiner's first fund increased from $7.46m in 1973 to $345.56m in 1986, an average return of 34.3% (although since not all the money was invested at once, the internal rate of return was higher).

It is interesting to note that nearly 95% of the fund's final value came from two investments: Genentech and Tandem Computers (a company specialising in network systems that could continue running even if several parts were either disrupted or shut down completely). So you could argue that they were extremely lucky. However, 10 out of the 17 investments made a positive return, and even if both Genentech and Tandem had failed, the final value would have been $19.2m, a respectable 7.5% annual return.

What you can learn from Kleiner Perkins

As noted in the last chapter, most ordinary investors can't invest directly in companies (though that may change with crowdfunding). In any case, it is almost impossible for ordinary shareholders to have a significant impact on the decisions that a company takes. The good news is that, with a bit of imagination and lateral thinking, several of Eugene Kleiner's observations about investing can be useful for those thinking about buying shares in both technology companies and fast-growing firms in general.

For example: Kleiner stated that, when it came to public offerings of stocks, "even turkeys can fly high in a strong wind". He also admitted that "venture capitalists will stop at nothing to copy success". In practice, this means that when there is a huge amount of enthusiasm about a technology, or when a new type of company is successful, venture capitalists will start pouring huge sums of money into copycat companies. At the same time, savvy investors will seek to cash in on the new enthusiasm by listing even mediocre fledgling companies in the same sector, confident that investors will be willing to pay a premium for these firms.

Naturally, most of these latter companies will prove to be poor investments. The internet has clearly changed the world (if not quite as fast as people expected) and quality companies like Amazon and Apple have been tremendous investments. However, during the 1999–2001 period some truly dire firms, like eToys.com, were brought to market – and saw their prices mushroom in the first few days of trading before falling quickly back to earth or even going bankrupt. Similar things have happened during other technology bubbles, right back to the railway mania of the 1850s.

Making sure that the potential market for a technology or product is big enough to support a company is also important, especially if it is going to face competition. Just because a company has developed an interesting product, it doesn't meant there is necessarily any commercial potential – you need to check.

Technology investors also need to have a view to future technology trends. It's not a good idea to invest in a company that ends up having its major product made obsolete by future innovation. As Kleiner put it: "try to avoid the $30,000 refrigerator". Conversely, certain products and services may need to be sold at a heavy discount, or even a loss, in order to create a market, as "there are two types of early adapters, those who buy and those who want the product given to them".

The classic example of a company that successfully followed such a strategy is Amazon. Between its floatation in 1997 and the end of 2001, it failed to turn a profit. Although its original business plan had stated that it wouldn't make money for several years, during the collapse of the tech bubble there was speculation that it might not be able to make interest payments. However, investors who stuck with the firm while it transformed retailing were rewarded by seeing the share price rise from $18 in May 1997 to over $11,600 exactly two decades later (adjusting for share splits), an annual return of 38% a year from a rise in the price alone.

Kleiner was also a big fan of boards of directors who "will give you better advice than your mother". Several studies, in various different countries, all suggest that good corporate governance can lead to higher stock returns. For example, Wolfgang Drobetz of the University of Basel found that buying German companies with high levels of corporate governance and shorting those that had bad corporate governance would have earned abnormal returns of 12% between 1998 and 2002. Similarly, Paul Gompers found in 2003 that during the 1990s a similar strategy for the US market would also have produced excess returns, this time nearly 9%.

RATING
EUGENE KLEINER
& TOM PERKINS

Performance: *While public records of returns are scarce, the evidence suggests that KPCB delivered a huge return to investors in the 1970s and 80s, even by the standards of venture capital companies. Perkins would also make a string of very successful investments, enabling him to accumulate a huge fortune. (★★★★★)*

Longevity: *While Kleiner was involved in KPCB for only 14 years, Perkins would be involved in technology investing for several decades. (★★★★)*

Influence: *KPCB did a huge amount to refine Doriot's model for venture capital investing. Indeed, many experts believe that Kleiner and Perkins were two of a handful of people who essentially created the Silicon Valley technology cluster. (★★★★)*

Ease of replication: *Unless you have a huge amount of capital to invest, most investors won't be able to get involved in early-stage venture capital investing. However, there are plenty of small-scale technology companies listed on the Nasdaq and AIM. (★★)*

Overall rating: 15 out of 20

CHAPTER 15
John Templeton

===

The Global Investor

Introduction

E VEN TODAY, INVESTORS in both Britain and America prefer to invest in their own stock markets. Indeed, 90% of shares held by individual American investors are listed on US exchanges, even though the US market accounts for only half of global stock market capitalisation. While you would expect investment professionals to be much less conservative, the average American mutual fund still only has one-quarter of its assets invested outside the US. British equity funds have half their assets invested in the FTSE, even though it accounts for a measly 7% share of global equities.

However, if you go back to the immediate postwar period, this 'home country bias' was even more pronounced. Indeed, the received wisdom at the time was that any foreign investment, above a token amount, was unacceptably risky. While lower transaction costs, better information and the rise of emerging markets have all played their part in making the investment world a smaller place, the success of those investment managers brave enough to venture overseas has also played its part in persuading the average investor to look beyond her nation's borders. One of the most well-known of them was John Templeton.

From poker player to
star fund manager

Born in Tennessee in 1912, Templeton attended Yale University, after teaching himself the mathematics needed to gain entry. When the fallout from the Great Depression meant his lawyer father was unable to pay his tuition, Templeton used his winnings from poker games to enable him to complete his studies. After graduating from Yale in 1934, he then went on to study at Oxford as a Rhodes Scholar. However, the thing that would make the biggest impression on him was a seven-month trip around the world after his studies at Oxford ended. This would involve Templeton visiting no fewer than 26 countries, including Germany, India, China and Japan.

After returning from his travels, Templeton got a job with the brokerage firm Fenner and Beane (later taken over by Merrill Lynch). He impressed his boss so much that a few years later he lent Templeton $10,000 ($171,000 at 2015 prices) in order to take over an investment advisory firm from someone who was retiring. Shortly after the start of the second world war, Templeton would invest a similar amount in every share on the New York Stock Exchange worth less than $1, including many companies then undergoing bankruptcy. Templeton claimed that these shares would be worth $40,000 ($548,000) by 1943.

Templeton and his partner would continue expanding his investment advisory business during the 1940s and 50s. However, he grew frustrated at the slow pace at which the firm was expanding and worked out that running a fund would allow him to make more money by getting a smaller slice of a much larger asset base. He was also attracted by the tax benefits that he could get from setting up a fund in Canada (which meant that his investors wouldn't have to pay capital gains tax twice). As a result, he decided to set up a mutual fund in 1954 as a way of reaching a large audience. Despite an unsuccessful attempt to sell it, along with his investment business in the 1960s, Templeton would manage it until his retirement in 1992, at which point the Templeton funds were sold to rival management company Franklin for a reported $913m.

His retirement, and the sale of the funds to Franklin, would allow him to devote much more of his time and energy to his philanthropic activities, which centred around examining the links between science and religion. However, he still stayed connected to the world of investing, helping out his successors at Templeton Growth and providing them with advice and guidance. At the same time he also managed his own money and those of a select group of private investors (most notably advising them to sell out of stocks just before the tech bubble burst in 2000).

Investing abroad – and against the herd

During his early years as an investment advisor, Templeton focused on trying to get a good return by getting his clients to change their exposure to shares depending on whether he thought the stock market was cheap or expensive. Specifically, he advised clients to increase their exposure to equities when firms were trading at low multiples of their trailing earnings and book value, and decrease their holdings of shares when price/earning ratios were higher. Indeed, when he returned to asset management in his later years he would save his clients a lot of money by getting them to sell their shares during the peak of the dotcom bubble. At the time this approach was called the 'Yale Method', though it is now popularly known as 'tactical asset allocation'.

However, Templeton took a very different approach when managing the Templeton Growth Fund. Indeed, he would abandon any attempt at asset allocation or market timing in favour of picking individual stocks that he felt would do well, irrespective of economic conditions. Of course, he kept a proportion of his fund's assets in cash in order to be able to deal with redemptions and be ready to meet new opportunities. However, this was very small, with at least 85–95% of the fund invested in shares at any one time.

The first book that Templeton read was *Security Analysis*, written by the dean of value investing, Benjamin Graham. As a result, he was very sympathetic to Graham's emphasis on finding bargains. He also agreed that it was important not to overpay for a company. However, he believed that some firms could still be bargains, even if they didn't look cheap on paper, provided their future growth prospects and profit margins were good enough to justify their valuation.

In order to find shares that were undervalued by the market, Templeton had to detach himself emotionally from the market consensus. He felt that this would be even more difficult if he remained physically close to Wall Street, as it would be easy for him to be swept up with the rest of the herd. Templeton therefore moved his offices away from New York. Initially this just involved moving to nearby New Jersey. However, in 1968 he would move even further – to the Bahamas in the Caribbean, taking up British citizenship (which would eventually result in him being knighted in 1987).

The most important part of his investment strategy was his global outlook. Templeton also felt that most investors reduced their chances of finding a good investment by cutting themselves off from overseas markets. Templeton therefore started putting large chunks of his funds into the shares of various companies outside the US. Indeed, at one point US shares accounted for just 16% of the total share portfolio, much lower than they would account for had the fund reflected the relative importance of the US.

Templeton's approach paid off handsomely. Between 1954 and 1992, the Templeton Growth Fund returned an annual average of 16%. This was substantially higher than the 11.8% delivered by the S&P 500 during the same period. Interestingly, his strongest performance came after 1969, returning 18.3% a year between 1969 and 1992 (beating the MSCI index by 6%). This success, combined with some savvy marketing, meant that the size of Templeton's funds mushroomed from $6m in 1955 to $751m by 1981.

By the time it and Templeton's other funds were sold to Franklin in 1992, they had a total of $13bn of assets under management.

Getting Japan right, wrong and right again

Nothing illustrates the strengths and weaknesses of Templeton's approach than his investments in Japan. In the postwar period, Japanese companies didn't appear to be particularly cheap. However, their idiosyncratic form of accounting meant that their actual profits were far higher than they appeared. As a result, they were in fact incredibly cheap. At the same time, Templeton realised that the Japanese economy was expanding at a tremendous rate and was extremely politically stable, reducing the risk that this growth would be disrupted or that the government would introduce punitive levels of taxation.

As a result, when Japan finally removed capital controls in the late 1960s (which had previously made it hard for foreign investors to buy Japanese shares), Templeton moved a great deal of the fund's money into the country. While Templeton didn't own any Japanese shares in 1964, five years later they would account for 18% of the portfolio, at a time when they were equivalent to 3% of global equities. By 1974 nearly half the portfolio was in Japanese shares, while the comparable amount for the MSCI world index would still only be 12%.

This coincided with a huge run-up in the value of the Nikkei, which shot up more than five and a half times in the 12 years from the start of 1968, an annual appreciation of around 15% a year, not counting dividends. This greatly helped his fund's performance during the 1970s. However, by the early 80s, the increase in share values meant that Japan was no longer cheap. As a result, Templeton cut back his exposure to the point that by 1989, the peak of the bubble, he didn't own any Japanese shares, even though they accounted for 40% of global equities by market cap.

Naturally, this early departure during the 1980s hurt the Templeton Fund's performance, though it didn't prevent it from beating the market. However, Templeton's fears were proved justified when the market peaked at the end of the 1989 and began to collapse. Despite a brief rally in the winter of 1990–1, it was down nearly 60% by the summer of 1992. Even today, 25 years after Templeton stepped down from directly managing his fund, the price level of the Nikkei is less than half the value it was at the peak of the bubble.

Importance of overseas investing

International investing is one of the areas where today's ordinary investor has it easier than John Templeton did. While he had to spend large amounts of time on planes, searching for opportunities, and had to deal with the bureaucracy surrounding international investing, large amounts of information on international countries and individual companies are available on the internet. Online trading has cut the cost and hassle of investing abroad, while many foreign companies have secondary listings on the British and American markets. What is more, country- and sector-specific exchange-traded funds provide a low-cost way to buy into foreign markets.

Of course, the one downside to the huge amount of information cascading through our computer and television screens is that it's harder to achieve emotional separation from Wall Street. Indeed, even if you are lucky enough to be able, like Templeton, to escape to the Caribbean, you will be bombarded with enough news and market gossip that you might as well be on Wall Street. Perhaps the answer is to be selective as to the information that you receive.

If you want to follow in Templeton's footsteps, it is also vital to be extremely patient. While buying an undervalued share and seeing it soar in value can be very satisfying, it can be equally frustrating to see it stagnate or even continue to fall in price. Of course, if it does take off, there will eventually come a point when it will no longer be cheap and you will have to sell it (as Templeton did with Japan). Indeed, the real test of a value investor is resisting the urge to follow the crowd into an overvalued market, like Japan in the late 1980s. Such an approach requires iron discipline, even if you are eventually proven right.

RATING
JOHN TEMPLETON

Performance: *Templeton beat the S&P 500 by over 4% over nearly four decades. He also grew the Templeton Growth Fund from a tiny fund into a $13bn behemoth.* (★★★★★)

Longevity: *Templeton was involved in investing from the mid-1930s through to his retirement in the early 1990s.* (★★★★★)

Influence: *While British investment trusts had been investing abroad since the 19th century, Templeton played a big role in encouraging American fund managers and private investors to consider foreign companies.* (★★★★)

Ease of replication: *There are a number of ETFs that allow you to gain broad exposure to a particular region, or a country. Many foreign companies have shares that are traded on British and/or American exchanges. However, buying and selling foreign shares directly gets more expensive the further you go from the main markets.* (★★)

Overall rating: 16 out of 20

Lindsell Train itself (which is not listed). Both these funds have outperformed the FTSE All-Share, which has returned only 121% (5% a year), including dividends, during this period. Between 2007 and 2016, Lindsell Train Global Equity rose by 194.3% (12.76%), compared with 74.1% for the FTSE (6.3%).

As a result of his success, the Lindsell Train Investment Trust now trades at a whopping premium of 70% to the value of its net asset value. In other words, investors value Nick Train's management skills so highly that they are willing to pay a 70% premium to the value of the shares in his portfolio (which at one point reached 70%), even though most investment trusts trade at a discount to the value of the portfolio. Indeed, Train has warned investors that he considers the premium to be excessive. Meanwhile, the more liquid Lindsell Train Global Equity fund also trades at its net asset value, with a small premium.

INVESTMENT STYLE

Nick Train's most successful investment was in the football club Manchester United, which he was still at GT Management. He bought the club during the 1990s (the club was floated in 1991). He saw that its name recognition and international fan power base set the sector to it. It would benefit hugely from the explosion in revenue from television money. During the 1990s, this prediction was proven correct, as the amount paid by television companies increased from about £60m to £170m a season by the end of the 1990s, thanks to the development of the Premier League. As a result, Train saw the value of his investment soar as the shares increased by over 30 times.

Another investment that has been extremely profitable has been in the clothing firm Burberry. In this case, Train kept track of it for a number of years before deciding to buy. While he greatly admired the quality of its products, he thought that it was too expensive, even for him. However, when it halved in price during the height of the financial crisis to £3.60, he started buying it, and then bought even more when it continued to fall to £2.60.

CHAPTER 16
Robert W. Wilson

The Short Seller

Introduction

ONE OF THE most controversial things in investing is the idea of short selling. Indeed, many people think that selling a share that you don't own in the hope that it will fall in price, enabling you to buy it back more cheaply, is immoral – profiting from the misfortune of others. Short sellers have also been blamed (usually with little justification) for causing individual stocks, or the entire stock market, to crash. Even today, there are restrictions on shorting the shares of companies that have fallen by a certain amount in value.

While many investors and traders have engaged in short selling, far fewer have put it at the core of their investment strategy. This is for two main reasons. Firstly, if you are betting against a company, the most that you can make on your investment is 100% (what you will make if the company's shares go to zero). In contrast, your losses are theoretically unlimited. Another reason is that, since shares have nearly always outperformed bonds and cash over extended periods, you are likely to lose money over the long run unless you have a particular talent for finding stocks to short.

As a result, those investors who have engaged in short selling have either only used it on a relatively limited number of occasions, like George Soros in the run-up to Black Wednesday and Jesse Livermore before the Wall Street Crash. Alternatively, they have used it in order to hedge out the impact of market fluctuations on their portfolio. Robert Wilson is one of the few exceptions to the rule, taking a large number of individual short positions over the 30 years he was actively invested in the markets, and using them to make money rather than merely managing risk.

Putting his investing before his day job

Robert Wilson was born in 1926 in Detroit. In 1946 he graduated from Amherst College with an economics degree. After spending a two-year stint at the University of Michigan Law School, he decided to drop out and get a job with the bank First Boston. After a brief period of mandatory army service, and another short period at First Boston, he decided to find a more permanent position in the trust section of the National Bank of Detroit. He would credit this time with teaching him about investing.

Indeed, Wilson was so eager to make his fortune that in 1956 he plunged $20,000 he had saved into the stock market. The problem was that he used borrowed money to enable him to buy more stocks, just before the stock market fell. This leverage meant that when the two stocks that he invested in – IBM and Houston Lighting & Power – temporarily fell, he was completely wiped out. Ironically both stocks would quickly recover and perform very well over the next decades.

In 1958 he received a $15,000 inheritance from his mother, allowing him to reinvest in the stock market. At the same time he took the decision to move to New York, where he worked for various investment funds, while managing his own money on the side for the next decade. By 1968 A.G. Becker, the company he was then working for, had become increasingly worried about the amount of leverage he was using in his own trading. They gave him an ultimatum: adopt a less aggressive strategy or find a new job. By then his own private account had grown so large that he decided to leave them.

The same year, he decided to set up his own hedge fund, Wilson and Associates. The fund was badly hit by the stock market downturn in the early 1970s, causing most of his investors to leave him. The fund quickly bounced back, enabling him to break even within a matter of months. However, angered by a perceived lack of faith, he returned all the money to his remaining investors and focused on his own investments (though he would later take part in some small external investment partnerships).

Wilson would continue actively managing his own money for the next 15 years. By 1986, feeling that the number of obvious investment opportunities had shrunk so much that he could no longer continue to keep beating the market, he decided that it was time to retire. As a result, he sold his active investments, moving day-to-day responsibility for his money to a group of fund managers. He also started small-scale philanthropy. By 2000, he decided to give the bulk of his fortune to a private charitable foundation. After his death in late 2013, the remainder of his fortune was given to charity.

Adding leverage to hedged investments

Wilson's strategy was to take long positions in stocks. He would then partially offset some of these long positions with carefully selected shorts. To boost returns, he then added leverage by using borrowed money to increase the amount of funds available for investment. Indeed, Roemer McPhee, Wilson's biographer, estimates that $4 out of every $5 that Wilson invested was borrowed. While the short positions reduced the impact that market fluctuations had, the increased leverage meant that if his long and short picks were wrong, even for a short period, he would lose a lot of money very fast.

Wilson's long positions were mainly in growth stocks. As a private investor he benefited from the fact that capital gains were taxed at much lower rates than the income that came from dividends. He also liked the fact that the stock prices of growth companies were more volatile than those of more conservative stocks, increasing the chance of a really large gain. In particular, Wilson liked two types of growth companies: those that were more innovative than their competitors, which allowed them to maintain both market share and margins; and those in industries that were growing very fast.

Robert Wilson's short positions can be grouped into three categories. Firstly, he shorted companies that he felt had been overhyped by brokers and other investors, who had driven their price far above what a rational investor should be expected to pay. Secondly, he liked to bet against firms that had done well but which he felt were vulnerable to competition, which would push down their margins and consequently their profits. Finally, Wilson also shorted companies that he felt were in serious trouble and were at risk of being driven into bankruptcy, which would drive down their prices to zero.

Turning a nest egg into a large fortune

Although Wilson's strategy was extremely risky, it seems to have succeeded beyond his wildest dreams. Starting out with an initial investment of $15,000 in 1958, the value of his portfolio reached $230m in 1986 – a compounded annual return of 40% a year. This was given a big jump start by the fact that his net worth rose tenfold between 1958 and 1960, and he also clearly added money from his day job to his portfolio (which distorted the figures further). Still, even if you exclude the leap in value over the first two years, a 32.6% annual return over 26 years is still outstanding, especially since the stock market dipped several times in the 60s and 70s.

From 1986, his net worth increased from $230m to a peak of $800m in 2000. This average annual return of 5.3% was obviously much less impressive, and highlights the problem with using external fund managers. However, it occurred at a time when he was already starting to give away money to various charities, which meant that he had to take money from his collected capital. Overall, the growth of his initial $15,000 investment into $800m over 42 years meant that his net worth grew at a rate of just under 30%, compared with the 12.9% return from the S&P 500 during that period.

Success on both the long and short sides

One of Wilson's main long investments was in the early computer company Datapoint. Wilson was attracted by the fact that the company's products, which consisted of computer terminals and early personal computers, were vastly superior to existing technology, and much more convenient for the firms that used them. He believed that this technological edge meant that Datapoint had huge room for growth. This proved to be correct, and even though the stock had already risen by a large amount before Wilson jumped in, he still made 14 times his money from 1969 to 1982.

Another example of a long investment that worked out was the restaurant chain Denny's. Wilson reasoned that the success of McDonald's showed that there was a huge demand for fast food. He also liked the fact that Denny's, which followed a very similar franchising strategy, had found a way to target a particular segment of the market (coffee and breakfasts, instead of burgers and fries) so it wouldn't be directly competing with McDonald's. What's more, it was less well known, so it was cheaper. Wilson bought the stock in the 1960s and made a lot of money out of it.

During the late 1970s the price of oil soared, reaching a peak of just under $40/barrel (equivalent to around $115/bl in inflation-adjusted terms) in early 1980. As a result, the shares of oil companies also greatly increased in value. Wilson believed that the oil price rise wasn't sustainable, and that many of the worst-run oil companies were extremely vulnerable to a fall in the price of crude. By the end of 1980 he was shorting a large number of oil companies. By the mid-80s oil was back down to nearly $10/barrel and many of the companies that Wilson had shorted ended up bankrupt.

Squeezed in Atlantic City

Despite Wilson's success, he is most remembered for one of his few blunders: the decision to short the hotel and casino chain Resorts International between 1976 and 1978. Wilson was drawn to Resorts because he felt that the hotel chain was poorly run and possibly inflating its earnings. Its decision to open a casino in Atlantic City made him even more bearish because he felt that few people would go to the town, which had a relatively cold and rainy climate. More cynically, he believed that regulatory action against organised crime would make it harder for the casino to collect gambling debts.

However, investors disagreed with his assessment, driving the stock from $8 a share to around $20. What's more, the opening proved to be a huge success as gamblers took advantage of the short distance from New York (compared to Vegas, a long airplane flight away). By June 1978 the stock price had reached $80. While Wilson bought some shares back at a loss, he still maintained a large short position. His rationale was that the price was too high and would fall back.

However, word of his losses spread around Wall Street and investors started a 'short squeeze'. This is where people buy a share that has been heavily shorted, in the expectation that the resulting price rise will force the short sellers to cover their positions, which in turn will push prices up even further.

This was further complicated by the fact that Wilson had chosen to go on an extended holiday, so he would return from a day sightseeing to find messages from his brokers urging him to cover. Eventually they said that unless he closed his position they would stop extending him any more credit. This forced him to give in and he covered the remainder of his position at $187 a share. His overall losses ended up being over $24m. However, a good performance in his long positions meant that he only lost $14m that year.

The eighth wonder
of the world

Virtually all experts agree that taking on huge amounts of leverage is a bad idea for the average investor, no matter the strategy. However, Wilson's success shows that short selling can be used to generate returns, rather simply as a hedge against the market rising. Indeed, a 2008 study by Ferhart Akbas of Texas A&M University noted that heavily shorted stocks tend to subsequently do worse than the overall market. This suggests that short sellers are generally savvy investors. Of course, the reason they tend to be so good is that they have to be at the top of their game if they are not to end up losing large sums of money.

Wilson's experience with Resorts International shows that even the best short sellers occasionally end up coming unstuck, whether because of the unpredictability of the market or because the initial idea was wrong or a combination of the two. Indeed, in some cases losses from short selling can be several times an initial investment.

It's also important to note that most of Wilson's ideas for investment originally came from the large number of brokers that he talked to on a daily basis. However, he then did his own research and analysis to determine whether they were worth following, ignoring or even going in the opposite direction.

Finally, the fact that Wilson was able to turn a nest egg into an unimaginable fortune over a long period shows the power of compound interest. As Albert Einstein famously put it, "Compound interest is the eighth wonder of the world. He who understands it, earns it, he who doesn't, pays it." Indeed, even if Wilson hadn't been so successful, and had instead only been able to follow the market, his $15,000 investment in 1958 would still have been worth nearly $2.5m by 2000, a very tidy sum.

RATING
ROBERT W. WILSON

Performance: *Wilson's early experience with leverage saw him being wiped out. His time running a hedge fund was also unhappy, even if he still ended up making money for his investors. However, turning $15,000 into $800m is nothing short of extraordinary, even if he probably topped up his investments with his Wall Street salary.* (★★★★★)

Longevity: *Wilson actively traded for over 25 years, and tried to grow his money for over four decades.* (★★★★★)

Influence: *Despite his huge success, Wilson remains a largely overlooked figure. Even today he is best known for the money that he lost on Resorts International.* (★★)

Ease of replication: *Both short selling and using huge leverage are extremely risky strategies and so not recommended for ordinary investors. The fact that he had to give up his day job to concentrate on his investments shows the amount of dedication required to successfully implement such a strategy.* (★★)

Overall rating: 14 out of 20

CHAPTER 17
Edward O. Thorp

═══

The Revenge of the Quants

Introduction

OVER THE LAST three decades there has been an explosion in the number of 'quants' or 'rocket scientists' in the financial sector. These people – usually with a background in science, mathematics or statistics – analyse large amounts of past data to find market anomalies. They then devise computer programs that automatically exploit these anomalies without the need for further human intervention. Supporters of this approach to investment argue that it is far more evidence-based and objective than traditional stock picking, which relies on received wisdom that may be out-of-date, and subjective human judgement.

Of course, critics counter by arguing that if you look at huge amounts of data, chances are that you'll come across some apparent anomalies by chance, even if they don't actually exist. Indeed, even if they did exist at one point, there's no guarantee that they will continue to persist, especially if other people are searching for them. They also point out that many scientists and mathematicians consider the task of sifting through financial data to be dull work, especially compared to more cutting-edge financial research. As a result, those that end up on Wall Street are those who aren't able to get more prestigious, or intellectually stimulating, roles elsewhere.

Even when the intellectual firepower is top-rate and the anomalies real, the use of mathematical models can inspire overconfidence. The classic case is the example of the hedge fund Long-Term Capital Management (LTCM). Founded in 1994 by a former head of bond trading at Salomon Brothers, along with two Nobel-Prize-winning economists, it initially used a large amount of leverage to make a huge amount of money through automated bond trading. However, the market disruption that occurred in the wake of the 1998 Russian default caused it to nearly go bankrupt, forcing the US Federal Reserve to organise a bailout.

Despite these criticisms, it is unlikely that the revolution in quantitative investing will be significantly reversed. Indeed, you could argue that the biggest threat to the rocket scientists comes not from traditional stock pickers or regulators but from developments in artificial intelligence. Some hedge funds (such as Sentient Technologies) are already devising programs that will come up with their own investment strategies, making the quants redundant. While there were several figures who played a key role in this development, one of the earliest investors to systematically use quantitative strategies was Edward O. Thorp.

From blackjack to the stock market

Edward Thorp was born in Chicago in 1932, though he and his family later moved to Lomita in California. High grades in chemistry and physics would win him a scholarship to University of California, Berkeley, though he would transfer to UCLA to complete his undergraduate studies. After completing his degree in chemistry, he embarked upon graduate studies in mathematics, getting his PhD in 1958. Meanwhile a visit to Vegas piqued his interest in the game of blackjack (also known as 21). While doing postdoctoral research at MIT he realised that if you adjusted your strategy to take into account the cards that had been previously dealt, it was possible to get a small edge over the casino.

Thorp published his findings to great acclaim and publicity in 1961. While many in the industry still expressed scepticism as to whether it was possible to consistently beat the casinos, several investors offered to back his ideas with hard money. The subsequent Vegas trips would make Thorp and his associates a lot of money, although they quickly found themselves banned from most casinos. (Thorp claims that one casino allegedly tried to spike his drinks while he was playing and even tampered with his car's accelerator.)

Thorp would go on to detail his strategies in the bestselling book *Beat the Dealer: A Winning Strategy for the Game of Twenty-One*, published in late 1962. This book has inspired many gamblers to attempt to follow in his footsteps. However, while card counting remains legal, casinos are allowed to take several counter-measures against anyone they suspect of doing this. This includes changing the rules of the game to move the odds in their favour (for instance, by lowering payouts on some bets) to simply banning suspected card counters from their premises.

Blackjack wasn't the only game that Thorp attempted to break. While still at MIT, he devised a machine that could predict the region of a roulette wheel in which a ball was likely to land. The problem was that, while preliminary Vegas trials showed that it could work well enough to generate consistent profits, the device was extremely fragile. Eventually, he decided that attempting to develop it further would consume too much of his time. As a result he abandoned the project, though not before developing what many computer scientists regard as the first wearable computer.

In the mid-1960s Thorp turned his attention to the stock market. Initially he would try to follow established investment strategies, reading Benjamin Graham's *Security Analysis* as well as several works on technical analysis and charting. However, his early stock market investments convinced him that he needed to take a more scientific and systematic approach. Attracted by the options market, he turned his attention to it, working out a way to consistently make money. In 1966, now professor of mathematics at the University of California, Irvine, he detailed his strategy in another bestseller, *Beat the Market: A Scientific Stock Market System*.

Initially Thorp just managed the money of friends, fellow academics and interested investors. However, a meeting with Warren Buffett, who was in the process of winding up his own fund, convinced Thorp that he should formally turn his various accounts into a hedge fund. He therefore set up Convertible Hedge Associates (later known as Princeton/Newport Partners) with Jay Regan, a stockbroker with the firm Butcher & Sherrerd. P/NP would become one of the first quantitative hedge funds, running from 1969 to 1989.

P/NP would be eventually wound down as the result of an investigation into two of its senior managers in the Princeton office, who were alleged to have helped the controversial junk bond investor and inside trader, Michael Milken, conceal his ownership of stock in a company. While their convictions were ultimately thrown out, and Thorp's side of the business was not involved, Thorp decided to part ways with Regan. Former investors persuaded him to set up a second fund, Ridgeline Partners, which ran for eight years from 1994. Thorp would also run a management account for a major company for ten years from 1992 to 2002.

During the 1990s, Thorp continued to pursue various projects, including acting as a freelance investment consultant. At the time of writing he is currently working on several biotechnology projects, including one that would allow corneas to be stored for longer before being transplanted.

Systematic and scientific investing

Thorp initially focused on warrants, long-term call options that allowed the owner to buy shares at a fixed price, devising a formula that allowed him to accurately price them. Further research revealed to him that the market frequently overvalued them. This allowed him to make a consistent profit by selling the most egregiously overpriced warrants short, while buying shares in the company to cap his downside risk. In the few cases where the warrants were underpriced, he would do the opposite, buying the warrants and shorting the shares.

Over the next two decades, P/NP would seek similar opportunities in other markets, starting with convertible bonds (bonds that could be converted into shares once they reached a certain price). It would also engage in pairs trading, identifying shares in the same sector that usually traded closely to each other but had temporarily diverged. The fund would then place bets on them converging again by buying the share that was doing badly and selling the one that had surged. A third strategy, popular during the volatile commodity markets of the early 1980s, was to exploit differences in the price of gold futures for delivery on different dates.

Another major idea was what Thorp called "statistical arbitrage". Thorp worked out the impact that various indicators (such as price momentum and price/earnings ratio) had on future returns. He then used these findings to produce a computer program that would not only rank stocks in order of attractiveness but then automatically buy those that the model expected to do well and short those that were expected to do badly. This hedging ensured that the returns weren't dependent on the direction of the overall market.

None of these strategies were new or novel. Convertible arbitrage had already existed for decades, while David Ricardo had engaged in a very primitive form of pairs trading in the early part of the 19th century. The idea of buying shares that are cheap relative to their earnings and book value was also an established strategy, especially since the publication of *The Intelligent Investor* in 1948. However, Thorp's use of computers to both identify opportunities and then automatically carry out large numbers of trades meant that P/NP's investments were much more systematic than those of other funds.

Of course, P/NP retained an element of human discretion, hiring expert bond traders from the investment bank Salomon Brothers, and investing in other hedge funds that it felt were particularly well run. While these detours into more conventional ways of making money were generally successful, Thorp ultimately believed that objective data-driven investing would produce superior results and avoid the stresses associated with managing large numbers of people, each of whom might have very different views on the market. As a result, Thorp's successor funds, Ridgeline Partners and the managed account, would rely almost completely on computer-generated investment decisions.

High returns, low risk

During its two decades of operations, P/NP was a runaway success. Despite the legal bills associated with the government investigation that led to its demise, and the way that it was wound up, it delivered strong returns throughout its life. $1,000 invested in P/NP when it was set up in November 1969 would have been worth $13,920 on December 1988 (when it stopped investing and started liquidating its assets). This equates to a net annual return of 15.1%, compared to 10.2% for the S&P 500. While this is impressive in itself, its performance was much less volatile than the market, never producing a negative return in a single year, even in 1974, when the market fell by 26.5%.

The managed account that Thorp ran between 1992 and 2002 would do even better, returning 18.2% over a decade, compared with only 7.8% for the market as a whole. This means that $10,000 invested in the fund would have turned into $54,800 by the end of the period. While these figures are gross – actual investors would have received less, thanks to fees – the accounts produced these gains with much less volatility. Indeed, Thorp claims that if you take the much lower risk into account, the account performed over five times better than the market as a whole.

Other good investments

P/NP's systematic style of investing makes it impossible to identify any one individual trade that was particularly lucrative. However, Thorp would make several good investments. From 1982 onwards, he would invest a lot of his wealth in shares in Warren Buffett's Berkshire Hathaway and recommend the stock to his friends. Realising that depositors in mutual savings and loans associations would be in line to get large allocations of shares at favourable prices, Thorp and his son made a lot of money from putting significant sums of money in those that were considering converting into public (i.e listed) companies and then withdrawing the money once the flotation process had been completed and they had received shares.

As an investment consultant, Thorp was asked to audit the records of an investor in Bernie Madoff's hedge fund – then seemingly producing strong returns with little or no risk. Growing suspicious of Madoff, Thorp looked closer, identifying widespread discrepancies between the number of option trades that Madoff was claiming to have carried out and the trading volumes stated in public records. However, while his conclusion that Madoff was running a Ponzi scheme was correct, and resulted in his client leaving the fund, others ignored Thorp's warnings. It wasn't until 18 years later, in December 2008, that Madoff turned himself into the authorities and confessed that the whole thing was a scam.

How to follow in Thorp's footsteps

If you want to directly emulate Thorp, you'll need to brush up your mathematical and computer programming skills. However, those of us less mathematically gifted can still follow his example by investing in 'smart beta' exchange-traded funds. These try to beat the market by following a specific investment strategy, such as value investing. However, unlike traditional funds they do so in a systematic way, rather than relying on a human manager. While they are more expensive than less-specialised ETFs, they are cheaper than active funds.

Even if you prefer a more qualitative approach to investing, you can learn a lot from Thorp's attitude to risk management. Not only did he believe in making sure that his downside risk was limited, and avoiding taking on too much leverage, he was a big fan of the Kelly Criterion, a system for deciding how much money you should stake on each individual bet (or investment). The basic idea is that your exposure depends on two issues: the perceived riskiness of an investment, and the expected returns. In short, you should only bet large amounts when you're sure that you have an edge. In effect, this is a slightly more sophisticated version of value investing's 'margin of safety'.

RATING

EDWARD O. THORP

Performance: *Both Thorp's funds and his private investments beat the market by a substantial amount.* (★★★★★)

Longevity: *Thorp's interest in the stock market began in the late 60s with his investigations into options trading, and lasted for over three decades with his involvement in various funds.* (★★★★★)

Influence: *Thorp played a big role in kick-starting the quantitative revolution, where banks and funds hired skilled mathematicians and scientists, who used computers to identify market anomalies and then exploited them.* (★★★★)

Ease of replication: *Spotting exploitable anomalies isn't easy, and takes time and a certain level of mathematical ability. In many cases, apparent anomalies are either too expensive to exploit (in terms of transaction costs) or are only a statistical mirage. While several smart beta ETFs have been set up to exploit some of the more basic quirks (such as the persistent outperformance of low-price-to-book value stocks), these remain extremely controversial.* (★★)

Overall rating: 16 out of 20

CHAPTER 18
John Maynard Keynes

===

The Stockpicking Economist

Introduction

E VEN IF YOU'RE not an economist, you'll probably have at least some idea of who John Maynard Keynes was. His economic theories enjoyed tremendous popularity during the immediate postwar era. While they fell out of fashion from the late 70s onwards, they have started to make a comeback since. Keynes's was famously caustic about financial markets, suggesting that when the "capital development of a country becomes a by-product of the activities of a casino, the job is likely to be ill-done". As well as supporting a transaction tax to discourage speculation, he even semi-seriously suggested that the government should "make the purchase of an investment permanent and indissoluble, like marriage".

Keynes was sceptical about the ability of anyone to consistently beat the market, arguing that, "investment based on genuine long-term expectation is so difficult today as to be scarcely practicable". Indeed, he noted that, "it is the long-term investor ... who will in practice come in for most criticism, wherever investment funds are managed by committees or boards or banks". In the world of money management, those who refused to follow the crowd were considered "eccentric, unconventional and rash" if they succeeded and could expect "little mercy" if they failed. In the Square Mile and Wall Street, "it is better for reputation to fail conventionally than to succeed unconventionally".

Given this rhetoric, you might imagine Keynes as the stereotype of an unworldly academic when it came to practical finance, keeping as much distance from stocks, bonds and other financial instruments as possible. In fact, he was speaking from a position of experience: he spent much of his adult life managing money, for both himself and other people and institutions. What's more, his story of repeated failure, followed by a period of eventual success, is one that the average investor can learn a lot from.

Combining academia and money-making

Born in Cambridge in 1883, Keynes won a scholarship to Eton, before gaining a place at Cambridge to study mathematics. After graduating in 1904, he spent a further two years doing various postgraduate studies, mainly in philosophy. Ironically, given his future fame, he would only formally study economics for one term. After spending two years working for the Indian Civil Service – which ran India from its London headquarters – frustrated at his lack of influence, he resigned and went back to his academic studies at Cambridge, initially supported by his father. While the plan was for him to focus on probability theory, he published his first article of economics in 1909 and was appointed a lecturer the same year.

From 1914 to 1919, Keynes played a key role in advising the British government as to how it should finance the war effort. This role led to him attending part of the Paris Peace Conference as a representative of the British Treasury, where the postwar settlement was thrashed out, as well as attending other meetings on the postwar treatment of Germany. His anger at the level of reparations that Germany would be expected to pay inspired him to write *The Economic Consequences of the Peace*, correctly predicting that it would increase the risk of a future conflict within 20 years. While it didn't have any impact on overall policy, it was an instant bestseller, establishing Keynes as a major public figure as well as making him a lot of money.

Keynes returned to Cambridge, spending the next 20 years of his life in academia. Between 1920 and 1939 he published a series of books, most notably *A Tract on Monetary Reform* (1923), *A Treatise on Money* (1930), *The Means to Prosperity* (1933) and *The General Theory of Employment, Interest and Money* (1936). All argued that fiscal policy (and some aspects of monetary policy, like interest rates) had a real impact on the level of output and employment in the economy, in contrast to the prevailing wisdom that it had little real impact. He argued that governments should therefore proactively use such policy to smooth the economic cycle, by stimulating the economy during periods of high unemployment.

In parallel with his academic life between the two wars, Keynes was actively involved in investment management. He was deeply involved with several pension funds and City trusts. These included three funds that he himself set up during the 1920s: the Independent Investment Company, A.D. Investment Trust and the P.R. Finance Company. He also had a role in advising the National Mutual Life Assurance Society and the Provincial Insurance Company on investment, though in both cases his decisions had to be approved by committee.

Keynes would also play the market for himself and his friends. Indeed, even before the first world war, he had been buying and selling shares for his own account, with his first recorded purchases in 1905. However, his postwar book royalties, money from his Bloomsbury circle, and even a loan from the merchant banker Sir Earnest Cassel, allowed him to engage in more aggressive speculation in the currency markets during the 1920s and 1930s.

Keynes's longest continuous involvement with managing money came from his role as bursar of King's College, Cambridge. Shortly after being appointed in 1919, he convinced the trustees to split the endowment money, which had previously been solely invested in property, giving him relatively free rein to invest how he liked. In practice this meant that he mainly invested in shares, with some exposure to commodity and currency futures. He would continue to manage this portfolio for over 25 years until his death in 1946.

During the second world war, Keynes reprised his first world war role of managing how the government should pay for wartime spending. He played a key role in the 1944 Bretton Woods Conference that determined the shape of the postwar financial system, including the creation of the International Monetary Fund. After the war finally ended, he spent the final months of his life persuading the United States to aid Britain's reconstruction by restructuring its wartime loans, allowing repayments to be spread over a much longer period, and by advancing fresh sums at favourable interest rates.

From asset allocation to stock picking

Initially Keynes believed that his main skill lay in his knowledge of macroeconomics. He therefore focused on the currency and commodity markets, using leverage to boost his potential returns, especially in terms of his private accounts. While such a speculative approach was inappropriate for the King's endowment, he employed what would now be called an asset allocation strategy, increasing the amount invested in shares when he felt that the economy was going to improve, but reducing his exposure to equities in anticipation of a recession (although his overall exposure to shares was much higher than for other comparable endowments at the time, which viewed stocks as too risky).

However, around 1932 he had become disillusioned with this approach. Instead, he switched to finding individual shares that he believed were undervalued, irrespective of the overall economic conditions. Like Benjamin Graham on the other side of the Atlantic, he would pay special attention to those companies that were selling for less than the value of their assets. David Chambers and Elroy Dimson suggest that after he changed his strategy in the early 1930s he was more likely to buy those companies that had experienced price declines, a contrarian approach.

Mediocre speculator but outstanding stock picker

Keynes's speculations were rather hit-and-miss. His early leveraged bets against the franc, lira and German reichsmark in 1919–20 made him a lot of money, encouraging his friends to invest alongside him. However, when the trades briefly went against him in early 1920, his high levels of leverage meant that he lost all his funds, along with the money that his Bloomsbury friends had put up, lured by his earlier success. He then took a loan of £5,000 from a financier to take similar positions, enabling him to repay his debts, and ending up with wealth equivalent to £1.1m at 2015 prices. However, his personal account was again wiped out in the Wall Street Crash in 1929.

His investment companies didn't do that well either. The AD Investment Trust was also destroyed by the Great Crash, though Keynes did at least have the common sense to sell his equity in the firm two years earlier, so at least it was a success for him. He ended his involvement with the investment decisions in 1927, so technically he can't be blamed for its failure. PR Finance Company was also badly hit, though thanks to a post-Crash shift in emphasis towards dividend-paying stocks it was able to grow enough to allow investors to eventually get their money back, something that can't be said for all investment funds at the time.

If Keynes's attempts at being a speculator enjoyed decidedly mixed results, his career managing the King's College endowment was much better. Over the 25 years from his appointment in 1921 until his death in early 1946, the discretionary part of the endowment returned a compounded average return of 14.41% a year, compared with only 8.96% for the stock market as a whole. This is equivalent to turning a £10,000 investment into £289,283, as opposed to £85,510. While the relatively subdued performance of the restricted part meant that the total endowment (excluding real estate) did only slightly better than the stock market, it experienced much lower volatility.

Interestingly, Keynes's performance from 1932–46 was much better than his performance from 1921–32. During the first 11 years (when he was employing an asset allocation strategy), the discretionary portfolio returned 10.1% versus 8.3% for the market. However, during the last 14 years, when he focused on buying cheap stocks, the gap between the discretionary portfolio and the market as a whole was much wider, with the former growing by 17.9% a year, compared to 9.6% for stocks in general. To put this another way, Keynes the market timer lagged the market in four out of 11 years in the 20s and early 30s, but Keynes the stock picker beat the market 12 out of 14 times thereafter.

Mining shares and car companies

One of Keynes's largest and most successful investments was in the gold miner Union Corporation. Originally, he bought into this company in 1933 as part of a move into South African gold miners. His rationale was that because these companies' revenues were linked to the gold price, but their costs (mainly wages) were linked to the rand, South Africa's decision to devalue would boost its profits and therefore the value of its shares. This proved to be the case and the value of Union's shares surged.

However, instead of selling, Keynes continued to profitably hold the stock through to his death in 1946. This was because he believed that it was still undervalued, since it was trading at a hefty discount of one-third to the value of its assets. What's more, many of these assets were in the form of liquid securities, which could be easily sold if it was broken up. In letters to friends he was also very positive about the quality of Union's management.

Another favourite stock, which also made Keynes a lot of money during the 1930s, was the British car manufacturer Austin Motors. As with Union Corporation, he chose this company because he felt that it offered relatively good value. In this case, he was attracted by the fact that it had a high earnings yield (i.e. a low price/earnings ratio), especially compared to other car firms. Indeed, he worked out that when you compared the number of cars that it sold to its market capitalisation, it was trading at around two-thirds the price of its American competitor General Motors.

Importance of flexibility

Keynes's disastrous experience as a speculator is additional evidence that it is very hard to make money in the market from short-term price movements. Despite his knowledge of economics, and the fact that he was ultimately correct about the overall direction of the market, his decision to use high levels of leverage left him vulnerable to short-term changes in the direction of the market. This is another illustration of the truth that it's not enough to be correct, you also need to know how to manage your money correctly so that you are not ruined by a sudden setback.

Contrary to myth, Keynes almost certainly didn't say "the market can stay irrational for longer that you can stay liquid". However, there is stronger evidence that he did say that "nothing is more suicidal than a rational investment policy in an irrational world" (though such a policy is what he did pursue after his change in strategy in the early 1930s). In any case, few can dispute his observation in the *General Theory* that, "an investor who proposes to ignore near-term market fluctuations needs greater resources for safety and must not operate on so large a scale, if at all, with borrowed money".

Keynes's attempt to follow a top-down asset allocation strategy in the first decade of his tenure as portfolio manager for King's endowment also produced mediocre returns. The problem with moving money in and out of the market is that such a strategy has to work extremely well to overcome the fact that in the medium- to long-run stocks generally tend to outperform less-risky assets, such as bonds and commodities. After Keynes switched to a much simpler strategy of focusing all his efforts on finding the stocks that offered the best value and opportunities, his returns were much bigger.

This also reveals a much wider lesson about the importance of being flexible. While it's never a good idea to abandon a strategy just because it doesn't immediately work or things go badly for a short while, you shouldn't indefinitely carry on with a failing strategy. After all, some people have a temperament or abilities that make them much more suited to one type than another. In that sense, Keynes's decision to admit to himself that he wasn't a very good trader, and instead switch to focusing on finding cheap shares, was the best decision that he made in his entire career.

RATING
JOHN MAYNARD KEYNES

Performance: *As bursar for King's College, Cambridge, Keynes's equity investments beat the market by a substantial amount, especially after 1932. However, his more speculative investments had a much more mixed track record.* (★★★★)

Longevity: *Keynes's involvement with King's investments lasted for 27 years, while he also engaged in other investment-related ventures.* (★★★★★)

Influence: *Although Keynes's work on economics had a big impact on both the subject and public policy, he was much less influential on the world of investment. Ironically, for someone who was most successful as a value investor, he is most known for his comparison of the stock market to a beauty contest.* (★★)

Ease of replication: *As he found out the hard way, his highly leveraged forays into the world of currency trading aren't really suited to private investors. However, his sensible strategy of buying undervalued stocks is much easier for investors to replicate.* (★★★)

Overall rating: 14 out of 20

CHAPTER 19
John 'Jack' Bogle

===

The Founder of Index Investing

Introduction

U P UNTIL NOW, all the investors that we've covered have produced large returns over an extended period (even if in a few cases they managed to lose a lot of it). However, the fact is that such managers are in a minority. Indeed, data compiled by Bank of America Merrill Lynch found that in 2016 only one in five large-cap US fund managers managed to beat the index. Over the long term, the situation is even worse. Indeed, one study by Standard & Poor's found that up to 99% of actively managed US funds failed to beat the index over ten years between 2006 and 2016.

These failings have prompted increased regulatory scrutiny of the fees that mutual funds charge (most recently by Britain's Financial Conduct Authority). However, it looks like the market is already dealing with this itself, with the last 15 years seeing an explosion in the amount of money managed passively by funds that simply follow an index. According to Morningstar, a third of mutual fund money in the US is managed this way, and experts think that this proportion will continue to increase. One man deserves the credit for creating this industry: Jack Bogle.

Poacher turned gamekeeper

John 'Jack' Bogle was born in Verona, New Jersey, only months before the Wall Street Crash, which wiped out his family's inheritance. He won a place at Princeton, doing a degree in economics. After reading an article about the Massachusetts Investors Trust, one of the first mutual funds, he became very interested in the industry, writing a dissertation on the topic. Echoing his future arguments, he was highly critical of the industry, arguing that funds charged too much, were too focused on marketing and would find it hard to beat the market over the long run.

Ironically, this thesis would lead to Bogle getting a job at Wellington Management Company, which ran the Wellington Fund, one of the largest mutual funds then in existence. Hired in 1951, Bogle would initially start by writing reports and doing various admin, public relations and marketing-related jobs. However, by 1955 he had been made assistant to the owner, Walter Morgan. This gave him the opportunity to get involved with all aspects of Wellington's business and put him in a prime position to persuade Morgan to allow Wellington to offer a fund that just specialised in shares, in contrast to the main fund which was split between several asset classes.

The Wellington Equity Fund (launched in 1958) was a success, with its second portfolio manager John Neff becoming a legend in his own right. However, the company continued to fall behind its competitors. Bogle decided that the best strategy was to merge Wellington with another investment management company, Thorndike, Doran, Paine & Lewis. While the aim was also to break into the lucrative pension fund market, the main reason was to benefit from TDPL's reputation as aggressive investors in growth stocks, which were then in fashion.

Initially, this worked well, and Wellington added even more funds. As a result, Bogle was appointed chairman of Wellington after Morgan retired. However, the firm was badly mauled by the market collapse in the early 1970s, which disproportionately hit growth stocks. At the same time relations between the various partners deteriorated to the point where they offered Bogle a choice of either leaving the firm outright or assuming an administrative function.

After several board meetings, they engineered a compromise. Bogle stepped down as chairman of Wellington Management Company, which would continue to provide investment advice to the funds (as they continue to do for some funds to this day). However, the funds would split from Wellington in all other respects, and would allow Bogle to set up his own division, which he named Vanguard, initially to provide administrative support. Bogle would serve as chairman of Vanguard from its foundation in 1975 to his retirement in 1999.

Buying the dartboard

Bogle's negative experience of trying to jumpstart growth through buying in expertise had turned him against the idea that managers could beat the stock market, as had his earlier studies at Princeton. At the same time, an increasing number of academics were arguing in favour of the 'efficient market hypothesis'. This stated that prices perfectly reflected all available information, and it was impossible for any individual to consistently beat the market, either through looking at past price movements or making predictions about the future. The only exception was if they had some insider knowledge, which was obviously illegal.

Paul Samuelson of MIT would go even further. In a famous 1974 article in the *Journal of Portfolio Management* entitled 'Challenge to Judgement', he argued that the poor performance of fund managers suggested that "some large foundation should set up an in-house portfolio that tracks the S&P 500 Index". Samuelson even called for the American Economic Association (the learned body for academic economists) to do so, though he admitted that "there may be less supernumerary wealth to be found among 20,000 economists than among 20,000 chiropractors".

Samuelson wasn't the only person to come up with the idea. Burton Malkiel of Princeton, in his bestselling book *A Random Walk Down Wall Street* (originally published in 1973), argued that since most stock pickers weren't as good as a blindfolded monkey selecting stocks by throwing darts at a newspaper's financial pages, you might as well buy the entire dartboard.

While Bogle wouldn't read the book until long after the fund was set up, Malkiel would later serve on Vanguard's board.

In any case, Bogle was so convinced by Samuelson's article that he used it to persuade Vanguard's directors to launch an index fund tracking the S&P 500. This fund was known as the First Index Investment Trust (now the Vanguard 500 Index Fund). Because it was not actively managed, Bogle was able to successfully argue that it didn't violate the agreement that Vanguard would stick to admin and stay out of the investment advice business.

First they laugh at you, then they copy you

The First Index Investment Trust met with a lot of industry resistance. Disliking his implicit critique of the industry, many on Wall Street called it "Bogle's Folly". Typical was the reaction of the then-Fidelity chairman Edward C. Johnson, who stated that, "I can't believe that the great mass of investors are going to be satisfied with just seeking average returns". Another fund manager called indexing "an avenue for seeking mediocrity". Probably the most extreme reaction came from some anonymous brokers who circulated one poster stating: '*Index Funds are UnAmerican*', and another asking the rhetorical question: '*Would you be happy with an average brain surgeon?*'

Given those attitudes, it's not surprising that the fund's public offering in August 1976 was a disaster. Backed by leading investment banks and brokerages, Bogle and his fellow directors expected to raise $150m ($624m in 2015 money). Instead they only managed to get $11.4m in investment. This prompted those organising the public offering to suggest that Bogle ditch the idea. However, Bogle refused. To get around the fact that $11.8m wasn't enough to cover the entire S&P 500, without incurring huge transaction costs, the fund decided to buy a representative sample of shares, enabling them to track the index very closely (later the fund would be big enough to allow them to buy the index outright).

This shaky start continued, as it took over six years and a merger with an actively managed fund for the assets under management to reach $100m. However, by 1987 the amount of money indexed reached $1bn. Meanwhile other companies slowly started to copy Vanguard, with Wells Fargo launching the first competitor fund in 1984 and Fidelity doing so in 1991. At the moment the Vanguard 500 alone has $26.4bn invested in it, while it is estimated that nearly $10trn in assets is passively managed.

Does passive investing work?

As the S&P study suggests, a simple index fund would have outperformed almost all actively managed funds over the last decade. However, defenders of active funds argue that this hasn't always been the case, with even Vanguard itself admitting that there have been periods where active management has beaten passive. For example, a 2014 paper put out by Vanguard noted that, while only 29% of US fund managers beat the averages during 1990–2000, this rose to 63% over the decade between 1999 and 2009. This suggests that while indexing is the best solution in bull markets, active management adds value when markets are flat or declining.

Still, over the longer run, the evidence suggests that passive funds generally do better. An investigation by the *Wall Street Journal*, using data from Wharton Research Data Services, found that only 20% of active large-company funds beat the S&P 500 over the last 25 years. Similarly, Vanguard's own data suggests that only around 20–25% of active funds beat the index over extended periods. Overall, data provided by Ben Johnson, director of passive funds research at Morningstar, suggests that over the past four decades the Vanguard 500 has beaten active US large-cap funds by an average of around 0.5% a year after fees are taken into account. Fifty basis points a year might not seem like a lot but it means that $10,000 invested with Vanguard in August 1976 would be worth $652,000, compared with $549,000 put into active funds.

Depressing or liberating?

On one level the fact that most fund managers fail to beat the market is depressing. After all, if the professionals can't do it, what hope does the ordinary investor have? However, you could put it another way, and argue that you don't have to produce huge returns in order to do better than most professionals. Indeed, if you don't want to spend time researching stocks, or sifting through funds to find the star performers, you can get a pretty decent return by just investing in a low-cost index fund. You can even combine passive and active investing, through exchange-traded funds. These are specialised index funds that are traded on the stock market like shares, meaning that you can use index funds to take bets on particular countries or sectors (though Bogle himself dislikes these funds because they encourage speculation).

Even if you don't want to ditch active management, the implosion of Bogle's career at Wellington demonstrates the perils of chasing fashionable sectors, especially given the stock market's tendency to revert to the mean over the long run. In his book *Bogle on Mutual Funds: New Perspectives for the Intelligent Investor* (1993), Bogle notes that investing in funds that had previously done the best would have *reduced* returns. Specifically, funds on the *Forbes* 'Honor Roll' (a list based on past performance) returned 11.2% a year between 1974 and 1992, compared with 12.5% for active funds as a whole and 13.1% for the stock market (minus a small transaction fee).

Another trick is to focus on active funds with the lowest cost. Asked to explain why he stuck with active fund management for so long, Bogle always maintained that in the 1950s the mutual fund industry kept costs at a reasonable level, but the rise of star fund managers and exploitative charges created an opening for indexing. Vanguard itself justifies running active funds by pointing out that the chances of beating the market rise to 40% for the cheapest funds. Ironically, as the next chapter will demonstrate, even Paul Samuelson, the man who inspired Bogle to start the first retail index fund, didn't really believe that the market was unbeatable.

RATING
JACK BOGLE

Performance: *By definition, indexing aims to produce returns that are only equal to the overall market. Indeed, because even index funds incur transaction costs and management charges, they technically lag the market by a small amount. However, the evidence suggests that the Vanguard fund has outperformed most actively managed equity funds over a long period.* (★★★)

Longevity: *From the time he was hired at Wellington in 1951, through to his retirement in 1999, Bogle's involvement with the fund industry lasted 44 years, over half of which was spent running Vanguard. Even today, he continues to write and comment about investing and the market.* (★★★★★)

Influence: *Despite intense scepticism, bordering on hostility, Bogle introduced retail investors to passive investing. Thanks to his persistence, trillions of dollars are invested in this way, with many experts predicting that active investing may end up being a niche area within a generation.* (★★★★★)

Ease of replication: *Putting money into an index fund is the simplest form of equity investment possible. Indeed, there are now a large range of low-cost passive funds, covering every conceivable market or sector.* (★★★★★)

Overall rating: 18 out of 20

CHAPTER 20
Paul Samuelson

≡

The Secret Investor

Introduction

B ORN IN 1915, Paul Samuelson got his degree in economics from the University of Chicago in 1935, followed by a master's and then a PhD in economics from Harvard in 1935 and 1941 respectively. Even before he had finished his doctorate, he had taken up a post as an assistant professor at MIT in 1940, becoming a full professor in 1949. His big breakthrough came when he wrote *Economics: An Introductory Analysis*, in 1948. This would prove to be one of the bestselling basic economics book of all time, and is still used as an introductory text on many college courses.

During a glittering academic career that only ended upon his death in 2009, Samuelson would make a huge contribution to all aspects of economics, finance and financial history. This would include trade policy, macroeconomics and the economics of public finance. He would also play a key role in encouraging economists to use high-level mathematical formulae to demonstrate how their theories worked. While this trend has got mixed reviews from many in the subject, who argue that it makes economics too detached from the real world, it would result in him being awarded the Nobel Prize in Economics in 1970 for his contribution "to raising the level of analysis in economic science".

Not only was Samuelson extremely influential in the development of economics as a science, he would also play an important role in shaping economic policy in the real world. During the second world war, he played an important role helping the US government to manage the labour market to ensure that both the needs of wartime production and the civilian economy were properly met. In the first seven years after the war ended, he advised the government on budgetary matters. From the 1960s onwards he would advise a range of US government agencies, including the US Treasury and the Federal Reserve, although his centrist approach to fiscal and monetary policy fell out of favour in the 1980s due to the rise of monetarist economists like Milton Friedman.

Random walk

One of Samuelson's biggest contributions to the world of investing was the idea of the 'random walk'. The French mathematician Louis Bachelier noticed that stock market prices moved in a very similar way to Brownian motion, the random movement of molecules. Having being alerted to Bachelier's work by a colleague, Samuelson concluded that the really interesting thing wasn't the specific similarities between the movement of stock prices and that of molecules, but the *randomness*. If it was impossible to discern any particular patterns that would predict the movement of stock prices, this suggested that most markets operated reasonably efficiently, so that all information was disseminated quickly and acted upon.

In turn, this meant that it would be impossible for an investor to consistently beat the market over the long run without taking additional risk, and that trying to do so was a waste of time. As noted in the last chapter, Samuelson argued that since the market was impossible to beat, it made sense to investors to buy a fund that tracked the market. This proved to be the big inspiration for John Bogle's index fund. While Samuelson didn't play any direct role in setting up the fund, he was a big advocate for it. Indeed, he repeatedly turned down an opportunity to become a director of Vanguard, not because he didn't believe in it, but because he believed that his support for index investing would seem less convincing if he had a direct financial interest in it.

Samuelson also pushed index investing during his time as a trustee of the pension fund TIAA-CREF. Thanks to opposition from other trustees, who wanted to continue with traditional active investment, he failed to get them to put all of their assets into index funds. However, he did persuade them to shift some of their assets into passive investments. He also got them to increase the amount of foreign shares that they held, further boosting performance.

Commodities Corporation

Samuelson might have been a big fan of efficient markets and passive investment, but that didn't stop him from being involved in more active investments. The most notable of these was in Commodities Corporation, a hedge fund set up in 1970 by one of Samuelson's PhD students, Helmut Weymar. Weymar's work on cocoa prices led him to believe that it was possible to predict the price of cocoa by looking at economic growth (which would impact on demand) and climatic variables (which would affect supply). Weymar initially used his studies to get a job at Nabisco, which made various chocolate biscuits and sweets. However, after several successful forays into the cocoa market he quickly realised that he could make a lot more money by becoming a professional speculator.

Samuelson invested $125,000 (later increased) in Commodities Corporation (CC), Weymar's hedge fund, which amounted to 5% of its start-up capital of $2.5m. He would also take a position on the fund's board, and agree, as he put it in a 2009 article written shortly before his death, to "become a monitor of traders". Samuelson would insist that he learned "to carefully abstain from influencing successful traders by offering them my macroeconomic views". However, Irwin Rosenblum, who served as the financial and administrative controller, claims that Samuelson took an extremely active role in board discussions, playing a key role in discussions on everything from operations to strategy, and even Weymar's view of particular markets.

Initially the firm struggled. During a period when corn prices were rising on fears of a crop blight, Weymar made a large bet on them falling, on the advice of an expert who believed that the problem was exaggerated.

However, when prices continued to rise further, Weymar panicked and sold his position, taking large losses, only to see prices subsequently tumble as the expert was proved correct. Combined with poor risk management, such bad trading decisions resulted in CC's capital quickly shrinking to $900,000 from $2.5m. Indeed, at one point in 1971 the firm was $100,000 away from being shut down completely.

Had this happened, Samuelson would have lost his entire investment, as Nabisco (the biggest investor) had a preferential agreement that gave it first call on any remaining capital. After much discussion the board agreed that risk controls be simplified and tightened, limiting the size of positions, especially those that went against the direction of the market. This heralded a wider shift away from making trades solely based on fundamental analysis towards an approach that relied much more on following trends (i.e. buying when prices were rising and selling when they were falling). According to Rosenblum, Samuelson initially resisted this change but went along with it after realising that it was the only way to survive.

These changes not only saved Commodities Corporation but enabled it to prosper. Over the next decade, CC would hire a number of star traders, most notably Michael Marcus and Bruce Kovner. It was very successful during the 1970s as inflation and rising interest rates led to markets that suited its trend-following approach. Indeed, by 1977, only four years after it began to make consistent profits, it was making so much money and employing so many people that it moved into its own dedicated building. Its capital also grew to around $30m, a twelvefold increase in less than a decade.

In the 1980s the fund was relatively less successful. The end of the commodities boom and the decline in inflation meant that many of the price trends that it had successfully exploited had disappeared. Some of its star traders began to leave for better opportunities, while the ones that stayed demanded higher salaries and bonuses, a drain on profits. Still, by 1989 it was successful enough to sell a 30% stake in itself for $80m, putting its total value at $267m. By the time the company was sold to Goldman

Sachs in 1997 for $100m, it was managing $1bn in assets, a 400-fold increase over 27 years.

Private investments

In addition to his formal roles at CC and TIAA-CREF, Samuelson made many private investments with the money from his Princeton salary, book royalties and other sources. Indeed, when his wife received an investment in the late 1930s he took advantage of the fact that shares were depressed to buy shares in solid companies that were trading at very low multiples of their earnings and offering generous dividend yields. Noticing that hotels were selling for a fraction of their construction price, even when you took the costs of refurbishment into account, he successfully invested in both the buildings directly and some of the early major national hotel chains.

Another extremely successful Samuelson investment was in the academic publisher Addison-Wesley. Having come into contact with them through their role as the main publisher of books by MIT academics, Samuelson was impressed enough to buy enough shares in the company and was invited on to the board. While he would eventually sell his stake after he got bored by the internal politics of the company, including a dispute between the founder and one of the major executives, he would hold on to the shares long enough to see the firm go from a small boutique to a major force in the publishing industry.

Samuelson also made a large investment in Berkshire Hathaway after being contacted in the late 1960s by Conrad Taff. Taff, who had studied at Columbia under Graham, wrote to Samuelson arguing that Buffett's success disproved the efficient market hypothesis. Intrigued, Samuelson did his own research, liked what he saw, and started buying Berkshire shares. Ironically, this was around the same time as Samuelson was testifying in Congress that the mutual fund industry was a waste of money for most investors. Between

1970 and Samuelson's death in 2009, each \$1,000 invested in Berkshire stock would have become \$2.12m, an annual return of more than 20%.

Of course, not all of Samuelson's investments worked out. Much to the amusement of his colleagues, he paid hundreds of dollars (roughly equivalent to thousands of dollars in today's money) for a tip sheet advising investors how to make money from options. Unsurprisingly, the majority of these proved to be duds. Interestingly, he implies that he largely gave up on putting additional money into specific stocks after Bogle launched his index fund, since indexing left him more time to focus on his day job.

Pretty efficient market

Samuelson's public support for indexing and efficient markets would seem to contradict his success at seeking out, and then taking advantage of, lucrative investment opportunities. Indeed, it is comforting to those of us trying to beat the market that even the man who played a large role in creating the efficient market hypothesis didn't seem to truly believe in it. In his final article Samuelson would seem to accept that the theory had flaws, stating that "a scarce subset of speculators can enjoy a 'positive alpha' during most of their active lives, meaning by those words risk-corrected extra returns as compared to 99% of the trading mob".

However, if it was possible for some people to beat the market, including by implication himself, he still argued that "there are no easy pickings in Wall Street". He cautioned that "such talents are hard to find. And they don't provide their services on the cheap. Lastly, even those guys' 'hot' hands often do turn cold". This is an important lesson that investors need to learn: even successful fund managers retire (like Peter Lynch), move to another firm (like Neil Woodford) or experience problems maintaining their success (like Anthony Bolton and even Warren Buffett).

Overall, the big lesson of Samuelson's career is that it is possible to beat the market in the long run, but only if you have an 'edge'. This doesn't necessarily mean access to inside information (which is illegal in most countries anyway), but it does mean that you have to have some sort of coherent investment strategy, even if it just involves buying a particular type of share. If you don't have such an edge, or such a strategy takes too much time and effort to implement, you would be better off, both in terms of returns and emotions, putting your money in an index fund.

Performance: *There are no audited records, but Samuelson clearly did make a lot of money from his investments in Commodities Corporation and Berkshire Hathaway. However, he would only have gotten an average return on his investments in Vanguard's index fund, and his attempt to play the options market don't seem to have been that successful.* (★★★★)

Longevity: *Paul Samuelson seems to have been involved in investing in some form or another since the late 1930s. Commodities Corporation lasted for just under 30 years, though it is unclear for how long Samuelson's direct involvement lasted.* (★★★★)

Influence: *Paul Samuelson played a key role in developing the efficient market hypothesis, which still has many adherents to this day, though obviously more in academic departments than on Wall Street. This in turn led to the development of index funds, which have changed the face of investing.* (★★★★★)

Ease of replication: *Setting up a hedge fund is beyond the resources of most private investors. Samuelson also seems to have found the internal politics of sitting on company boards too stressful. Buying into a fund like Berkshire Hathaway is relatively straightforward, though there are a limited number of exceptional fund managers such as Warren Buffett out there.* (★★★)

Overall rating: 16 out of 20

CONCLUSION
Lessons of the Superinvestors

W E'VE NOW LOOKED at the biographies, strategies and the best (and worst) investments of 20 great investors, as well as what their experiences can teach us. Here are the top ten lessons that, in my view, other investors can learn from them and apply to their own investing and trading.

1. The market can be beaten

The experiences of the superinvestors (excluding Jack Bogle) teach us that it is possible to consistently beat the market over an extended period of time. Of course, some academics still believe that markets are always perfectly efficient and the market can't be beaten. However, the large number of apparent anomalies picked up by both academics and quantitative hedge fund managers, as well as the market gyrations experienced during 2000–2 and 2007–9 means that other models, such as behavioural economics, are gaining ground even within the ivory towers of academia. Even academics have shifted towards Paul Samuelson's compromise position outlined in his final article: that the market isn't perfectly efficient and is beatable, but that it is very difficult to do so in practice.

Many of the investors featured in this book were extremely intelligent people, with several having an Oxbridge or Ivy League education (or equivalent). However, a surprising number came from more modest educational backgrounds, with David Ricardo and Jesse Livermore leaving school at a young age (though this was at a time when few people went to university). Interestingly, barely more than half the investors in this hall of fame formally studied economics, finance or business. This suggests that a good training in the humanities or hard sciences can be just as useful to the investor.

While most of the investors profiled are retired or no longer alive, around a quarter are still active in the world of investment, with Warren Buffett, Nick Train and Neil Woodford still running large sums of money. While Buffett's performance has been lacklustre in recent years, Nick Train and Neil Woodford continue to outperform. This suggests that even in today's liquid, computerised markets, where information moves around the world in the blink of an eye, there are still a lot of opportunities out there for savvy investors, including old-fashioned stock pickers.

2. There are many roads to investment success

It's true that some investment strategies stand a better chance of success than others. For example, studies have shown that, over extended periods of time, fund managers who focus on buying cheap shares tend to do better on average than those funds and trusts that try to buy into fast-growing companies. The returns from certain types of venture capital tend to be much higher than the stock market as a whole, while a large percentage of short-term traders end up making little money, especially if they are trading with their own funds. However, the variety of approaches successfully employed by the 20 investors in this book demonstrates that there are multiple ways to beat the market.

Indeed, even those investors who had the same overall approach still had an individual take on it. A good illustration of this is the four growth investors profiled: Philip Fisher, T. Rowe Price, Peter Lynch and Nick Train. As well as running money in very different periods, they each had a preference for different types of company. Philip Fisher's approach tended to focus on technology companies that spent large sums on research and development. T. Rowe Price liked firms in sectors that were fast-growing. Peter Lynch tended to prefer individual companies rather than sectors (though in practice a lot of his investments ended up being in a small number of industries). And Nick Train focuses on brands.

Because there are multiple routes to success, the best idea is to find a strategy that matches your skills and resources, rather than adopting an approach that might be completely inappropriate. For example, if you don't have much spare time and have little tolerance for risk, short-term trading might not be for you, even if you feel inspired by Jesse Livermore's career. Similarly, if you would rather try and find the next Google or Apple than go through reams of unfashionable and poorly performing companies in the hope of finding a bargain, you might be better off focusing on the great venture capital investors rather than trying to copy Benjamin Graham.

3. Be flexible...

A surprising number of the great investors profiled in the book changed, or at least modified, their approaches as their investing careers developed. The most obvious example of this is John Maynard Keynes, who eventually abandoned both asset allocation and leveraged currency trading in favour of becoming an extremely successful value investor. Robert Wilson originally started short selling as a way to reduce risk after a market dip wiped out his initial stock portfolio, and then quickly developed it into a strategy that made money in its own right.

Even those who maintained their overall approach throughout their careers were willing to make exceptions if the opportunity was good enough. A classic example of this is Benjamin Graham's decision to stick with his investment in GEICO long after it ceased to be a value stock. As a growth investor, Nick Train focuses on the quality of the underlying company, rather than the price at which the share is trading. However, this didn't stop him taking advantage of the fall in Burberry's stock price in the immediate aftermath of the financial crisis of 2008 to scoop it up cheaply, and he continues to hold it even though it has soared in price.

Perhaps the best example of someone who didn't let his views restrict his investment behaviour is Paul Samuelson. Even when he started down the research path that would culminate in him (and others) coming up with the efficient market hypothesis, he would still actively invest his money, and his advocacy of passive investing didn't stop him being involved with the very active management of Commodities Corporation. His decision to respond to a letter from one of Buffett's fans by investigating Buffett (rather than simply ignoring the letter), which ultimately led him to buy shares in Berkshire Hathaway, shows how being open-minded can help you make money.

4. ...but not too flexible

While flexibility can be useful, too much of it can be dangerous. It's one thing to ditch a strategy that clearly isn't working, but changing it on a whim can lead to sloppy decision-making that can get you into trouble. One big problem is that the skills required for one type of investing don't always work in a different context. For example, successful traders need to be fleet-footed and ruthless about closing losing positions. In contrast, venture capitalists need huge reserves of patience as it may take years of losses for a company to start to be profitable.

As a result, whenever traders get involved in long-term investments, or venture capitalists get involved in short-term trading, it usually ends badly. Getting emotionally involved in an investment can also make things worse. George Soros's decision to suddenly put a large sum of money into a privately listed (and therefore illiquid) Russian company, for reasons that were more philanthropic than economic, ended up costing him a lot of money. Similarly, Jesse Livermore would admit that his investments in various private schemes that were suggested by his friends and acquaintances played a large part in the decline of his fortune that had been amassed through careful trading.

The same can apply when picking funds to invest in. Investing with Fidelity Special Situations when it was run by Anthony Bolton would have made you a lot of money. However, those who followed his move to China would have experienced a lot of turbulence, even if they would have ended up slightly ahead in the end. Indeed, those who piled in after the first few good months would have seen the value of their investment plunge. Bolton admitted that the methods and assumptions that enabled him to prosper with British companies simply didn't work in an emerging market, where fraud was rampant and the needs of shareholders came a distant second to the whims of management.

In this regard it will be interesting to see how Neil Woodford's decision to launch a Patient Capital Trust (long-term venture capital fund) pans out. While the share price of the investment trust has lagged the market, such investments take a long time to show meaningful results.

5. Successful investing
requires an edge

Whether they found a successful strategy and stuck with it, or experimented until they found one that consistently worked, all the investors profiled had some 'edge' that enabled them to beat the market. This ranged from Jesse Livermore's ability to use past price patterns to predict future price movements to John Templeton's awareness that there were far more undervalued companies in the rest of the world compared to America on its own. Having an edge is important, simply because the stock market is what theorists like to call a 'zero-sum game'. As Paul Samuelson pointed out, for one person to outperform the average, someone else must underperform.

Indeed, because buying and selling shares incurs transaction costs, active investing can be seen as a negative-sum game (in that the two parties of a share transaction end up collectively worse off than if it had not taken place). This doesn't mean that active investment is necessarily a bad idea. Just as Edward Thorp was able to make money by overcoming the house's edge in blackjack, a shrewd investor is more than able to compensate for the costs of trading. However, if you don't have an edge (and one that is good enough to overcome the associated transaction costs) then you are better off minimising the 'croupier's take' by sticking your money in a low-cost index fund.

A small edge frequently turns out not to be enough to make money. As Benjamin Graham pointed out, valuation is always an inexact science since some assets can't be objectively quantified and human judgement is always fallible. If you think that something is only slightly undervalued, there is a good chance that you, rather than the market, have got it wrong. However, if you think that something is extremely undervalued, then even if you've made some errors you still stand a decent chance of making money.

6. When you do have an edge, bet big

Trading without an edge, or where the potential reward is relatively small, is a poor idea. However, when an opportunity to make a lot of money comes up, you should take the opportunity to put a large chunk of your portfolio into it. Most of the superinvestors tended to have portfolios that were much more concentrated than their peers, because they felt that there were only a limited number of great opportunities. Of course, there are exceptions to this rule, with Peter Lynch owning shares in a large number of different companies, but even then many of the companies that he invested in tended to operate in the same industries.

Even those traders who made their fortunes by grinding out a steady stream of small profits, like David Ricardo and Jesse Livermore, were willing to be much more aggressive at certain points in their careers. For example, Ricardo staked his entire fortune on the outcome of the Battle of Waterloo. Livermore also made several big bets, most notably his decision to short the stock market shortly before the Wall Street Crash. Of course, both Ricardo and Livermore only made these huge investments when they were absolutely sure that they would pay off.

Warren Buffett famously used the analogy of someone playing baseball. While mediocre baseball players will swing at everything, the best will wait until the ideal pitch comes along, which they can hit for a home run. Of course, investors are in an even better position than baseball players because there's no possibility of them being struck out, no matter how many pitches they allow to pass them by. Similarly, Edward Thorp bet heavily when his blackjack card-counting system indicated that the odds were in his favour, and scaled his bets right down to the minimum when they weren't.

7. Have an exit strategy

Deciding when to buy, or open a position, is clearly important. However, in some cases picking the correct time to sell, or cover a short position, can also play a huge role in determining how much money you can make from a trade. Sell a winning position too soon and you can pass up the opportunity of large profits, as Warren Buffett did with his initial investment in GEICO in the 1950s. Conversely, holding on to a losing position for too long can result in a minor loss turning into a disaster, as memorably happened in the case of Robert Wilson and Resorts International.

However, while many traders live by the adage of 'sell your losers and let your winners run', this strategy also has its risks. Indeed, those who prematurely bail out of a losing position can end up sitting on the sidelines in frustration as it subsequently soars (or falls in the case of a short). Conversely both Warren Buffett and Robert Wilson seemed to have won long-term success by accepting the occasional short-term reversal in favour of long-term performance. Indeed, Warren Buffett famously argued that investors should welcome declines in the price of their shares, just as consumers like a decline in the price of goods, because it allows them to add to their holdings.

The overall lesson seems to be that whatever exit strategy you end up adopting, it's vital to have some sort of plan. Such a plan needs to be appropriate to the time frame of your investment, the amount of risk that you're willing to take, and your ability to ride out periods of poor performance.

8. Ordinary investors have some advantages

With the notable exception of Jesse Livermore, most of the other superinvestors were involved in hedge funds, investment trusts or other types of investment vehicles that managed other people's money. This meant that in theory they could either be removed from their positions, or had the threat of investors withdrawing their money from their control. It also meant that they faced various restrictions on how they invested their money. While all of them managed to prosper, the restrictions clearly had a negative impact on their ability to make money.

Neil Woodford admits that he came under a lot of pressure to buy into technology shares during the height of the technology bubble, and his refusal to do so nearly cost him his job. This was even though his belief that those shares were overpriced was proved correct by subsequent events. Keynes was extremely bitter about the extent to which the investment committees that he was on encouraged groupthink and discouraged original thinking. Robert Wilson disliked running a hedge fund so much that he closed it, returning his money to investors.

It's not just the threat of being fired, or the need to pass investment ideas through a committee before they are approved, which can hinder professional managers. Mutual funds and closed-ended investment companies (or unit trust and investment trusts in the UK) have to obey certain regulations, which limit their ability to concentrate their portfolios. For example, Peter Lynch stated that he would have had far fewer (but bigger) individual positions if it wasn't for rules effectively stopping him investing more than 10% of Magellan's portfolio in any one company. He has also stated that his funds for corporate clients did better because they weren't so restricted.

Of course, professionals do have some advantages over ordinary investors. These include teams of analysts at their beck and call, and ready access to company executives. They also have the luxury of being able to spend all their time thinking about investments, rather than trying to make decisions during their spare time. It's also very hard for retail investors to invest in privately listed companies, especially those that are in the early stages of being set up. Still, private investors have a lot more freedom to take positions that go against the consensus of the market, and to make big bets and not have someone breathing down their necks. These factors help level the playing field somewhat, though only if you take advantage of them.

9. Big isn't always beautiful

In some respects professionals benefit from having a large amount of money under their control. Fixed costs, like research and admin, can be spread over a greater asset base, cutting the amount that each individual investor has to pay. Having a large amount of assets can also enable professionals to influence company policy at the board level. However, there are also disadvantages as well. Unless the manager wants to spread their investments across a wider range of companies, with possible negative consequences for returns, having a large asset base effectively stops managers from investing in companies below a certain size.

Take the example of a fund with £10bn in assets. Assuming that the manager wants to invest in a maximum of 40 companies, that means an average investment of £250m each. Since no manager will want to buy more than 10% of a company (because this makes it hard for the manager to buy and sell shares without moving the price), this means that the minimum market cap is £2.5bn, just under the size of the smallest company in the FTSE 100. This limits the manager to blue-chip companies, making it hard to make the contrarian investments that will generate outsize returns. After all, you can't beat the market if you are the market.

The classic case of a manager who has become too big to succeed is Warren Buffett. It's no coincidence that he has struggled to beat the market at the same time as the market cap of Berkshire Hathaway has reached hundreds of billions of dollars. Indeed, he has repeatedly stated that if he were back to managing millions of dollars, he would be able to make the sort of deep-value investments in obscure companies that allowed him to generate huge returns during the 1950s and 60s when he was running BPL. Of course, the smaller investor is able to invest in a wide range of companies, including tiny fledgling firms.

10. It's good to have some distance from the crowd

One thing that may cause surprise is the fact that the majority of the superinvestors located their funds or investment offices outside both London and New York, the two major global financial centres. In the case of Georges Doriot and Eugene Kleiner and Tom Perkins this can be explained by the fact that they wanted to be close to the industries that they were investing in. Similarly, Peter Lynch worked out of Boston because that's where Fidelity's offices were. However, it is less obvious why Warren Buffett chose to locate himself in Omaha, John Templeton in the Bahamas, Neil Woodford in Oxford or Edward Thorp in Newport, California.

Part of the reason must be a desire to keep physical and emotional distance from the Wall Street (or City) consensus. This distance allows an investor to see things with fresh eyes and therefore avoid making the same investments that everyone else is making. Naturally, this also applies to the ordinary investor. On the one hand, the rise of 24-hour financial television and financial websites means that you have access to the same information as the professional. However, if you're not careful then you can easily succumb to Wall Street (or City of London) groupthink.

It's therefore a sensible idea to take the occasional step back now and then. The important thing is to make sure that you're exposed to other views and information that isn't just the daily chatter of the market.

The best superinvestor?

As well as detailing the careers of 20 exceptional investors, and seeing what lessons can be learned from them, the other aim of this book was to find out which of them deserves to be considered the best of all time. While all of them are clearly exceptional, four stand out from the crowd: Philip Fisher, Warren Buffett, Jack Bogle and Benjamin Graham. Philip Fisher and Warren Buffett have 17 points each in the book's star-rating system (out of a possible 20), while Bogle and Graham have 18.

Fisher made a major contribution to investing with his writings on growth investing. He also had a long career managing other people's money and advising them about their investments. His idea of finding a small number of companies with the potential to grow at a fast rate and then holding them for long periods of time has an obvious appeal to time-strapped investors. However, few firms meet those criteria, and his focus was on research-intensive technology companies, not the easiest sector to understand. Additionally, detailed information on his returns isn't available, though from his stock selections they were clearly well above the average.

Buffett has produced exceptional returns over at least five of the last six decades (even if his recent results have been relatively disappointing). However, while many fund managers cite him as an influence, its hard to pinpoint what his style truly is: with a shift from deep value investing during the 1950s and 60s, to putting Berkshire's money in blue-chip stocks and stakes in private firms today. The latter strategy of buying stakes in unlisted companies (or buying listed companies and taking them private) is clearly not something that the average investor can copy.

Despite a slow start, Bogle's development of the index fund has ended up having a major impact on the entire investment industry over the four decades since its creation. Indeed, it may end up being its future. If you haven't got the time to do any research on investments, it may well be the best solution for you. However, the big problem with passive investing is that it throws away any opportunity for above-average returns (though 'smart-beta' funds are emerging which aim to deliver the benefits of active management for much lower costs). If you want to be pedantic, indexing will always lag the market because of transaction costs.

In my opinion, the best investor of all time is Benjamin Graham. He doesn't quite get a perfect score, since his record was dented by the Wall Street Crash and boosted by his investment in GEICO (which went against his rules). Value investing isn't quite as simple as buying an index fund. However, over his long and eventful career he beat the market by a large amount and had a massive influence on everyone from Warren Buffett to Anthony Bolton and others. The idea of buying shares in companies that are selling for less than the value of their net assets is a simple yet powerful strategy that is backed up by a lot of evidence.

BIBLIOGRAPHY

A. Published books

Arnold, Glen, *The Great Investors: Lessons on Investing from Master Traders*, (Harlow, 2011)

Benello, Allen C. et al, *Concentrated Investing: Strategies of the World's Greatest Concentrated Value Investors*, (Hoboken, 2016)

Bogle, John C., *Bogle on Mutual Funds: New Perspectives for the Intelligent Investor*, (Hoboken, 2015)

Bogle, John C., *The Clash of the Cultures: Investment versus Speculation*, (Hoboken, 2012)

Bolton, Anthony, *Investing Against the Tide: Lessons from a Life Running Money*, (Harlow, 2009)

Bolton, Anthony, *Investing with Anthony Bolton: The Anatomy of a Stock Market Winner* (2nd ed), (Petersfield, 2006)

Braham, Lewis, *The House that Bogle Built: How John Bogle and Vanguard Reinvented the Mutual Fund Industry*, (New York, 2011)

Carlen, Joe, *The Einstein of Money: The Life and Timeless Financial Wisdom of Benjamin Graham*, (New York, 2012)

Cathcart, Brian, *The News From Waterloo: The Race to Tell Britain of Wellington's Victory*, (London, 2015)

Cunningham, Lawrence A. (ed), *The Essays of Warren Buffett: Lessons for Investors and Managers*, (Singapore, 2014)

Fisher, Ken (ed), *Common Stocks and Uncommon Profits and Other Writings by Philip A. Fisher*, (Hoboken, 2003)

Golis, Christopher, *Enterprise and Venture Capital: A Business Builder's and Investor's Handbook*, (New York, 2002)

Graham, Benjamin, *The Intelligent Investor: The Classic Text on Value Investing* [1949 ed], (New York, 2015)

Graham, Benjamin with Zewig, Jason, *The Intelligent Investor: The Definitive Book on Value Investing – A Book of Practical Counsel* [revised ed], (New York 2003)

Gosling, Lawrence with Wallace, Jane, *Intelligent Investors: How Top Fund Managers Think About Investing Our Money*, (Dagenham, 2015)

Greenwald, Bruce et al, *Value Investing: From Graham to Buffett and Beyond*, (Hoboken, 2001)

Gupta, Udayan (ed), *The First Venture Capitalist: Georges Doriot on Leadership, Capital & Business Organization*, (Calgary, 2004)

Hagstrom, Robert G., *The Warren Buffett Way: Investment Strategies of the World's Greatest Investor*, (New York, 1997)

Lefèvre, Edwin, *Reminiscences of a Stock Operator*, (New York, 1994)

Livermore, Jesse with Smitten, Richard, *How to Trade in Stocks: The Classic Formula for Understanding Timing, Money Management, And Emotional Control*, (London, 2001)

Lowenstein, Roger, *Buffett: The Making of An American Capitalist*, (New York, 2001)

Lynch, Peter, *Beating the Street: The Bestselling Author of One Up on Wall Street Shows You How to Pick Winning Stocks and Develop a Strategy for Mutual Funds*, (New York, 1994)

Lynch, Peter with Rothchild, John, *One Up On Wall Street: How to Use What You Already Know to Make Money in The Market*, (New York, 2000)

Malkiel, Burton G., *A Random Walk Down Wall Street: The Time-Tested Strategy for Successful Investing* [11th ed], (New York, 2016)

Mallaby, Sebastian, *More Money than God: Hedge Funds and the Making of a New Elite*, (London, 2011)

McPhee, Roemer, *Killing the Market: Legendary Investor Robert W. Wilson*, (New York, 2016)

Miller, Jeremy, *Warren Buffett's Ground Rules: Words of Wisdom from the Partnership Letters of the World's Greatest Investor*, (London, 2016)

Morton, James, *Investing with the Grand Masters: Insights from Britain's Greatest Investment Minds*, (London, 1997)

Morris, Edward, *Wall Streeters: The Creators and Corruptors of American Finance*, (New York, 2015)

Patterson, Scott, *The Quants: The Maths Geniuses who Brought Down Wall Street*, (London, 2011)

Perkins, Tom, *Valley Boy: The Education of Tom Perkins*, (London, 2007)

Price Jr, T. Rowe, *Picking Growth Stocks*, (New York, 1939)

Rosenblum, Irwin, Up, *Down, Up, Down, Up: My Career at Commodities Corporation*, (Bloomington, 2003)

Ross, Nick, *Lessons from the Legends of Wall Street: How Warren Buffett, Benjamin Graham, Phil Fisher, T. Rowe Price and John Templeton Can Help You Grow Rich*, (New York, 2000)

Slater, Robert, *Soros: The World's Most Influential Investor*, (New York, 2009)

Smitten, Richard, *Jesse Livermore: World's Greatest Stock Trader*, (New York, 2001)

Schroeder, Alice, *The Snowball: Warren Buffett and the Business of Life*, (London, 2009)

Schwager, Jack D., *Hedge Fund Wizards: How Winning Traders Win*, (Hoboken, 2012)

Schwager, Jack D., *Market Wizards: Interviews with Top Traders*, (Hoboken, 2012)

Skidelsky, Robert, *John Maynard Keynes, Volume 1: Hopes Betrayed 1883–1920*, (London, 1992)

Skidelsky, Robert, *John Maynard Keynes, Volume 2: The Economist as Saviour, 1920–1937*, (London, 1994)

Steinhardt, Michael, *No Bull: My Life In And Out of Markets*, (New York, 2001)

Soros, George, *The Alchemy of Finance: Reading the Mind of the Market*, (Hoboken, 2003)

Sraffa, Piero (ed), *The Works and Correspondence of David Ricardo: Volume VI, Letters 1810–1815*, (Indianapolis, 2004)

Sraffa, Piero (ed), *The Works and Correspondence of David Ricardo: Volume X, Biographical Miscellany*, (Indianapolis, 2004)

Szenberg, Michael et al, *Paul Samuelson: On Being An Economist*, (New York, 2005)

Thorp, Edward O., *A Man for All Markets: Beating the Odds, from Las Vegas to Wall Street*, (London, 2017)

Train, John, *Money Masters of Our Time*, (New York, 2000)

Weatherall, D., *David Ricardo: A Biography* (The Hague, 1976)

B. Journal articles and working papers

Bauer, Rob (et al), 'International Evidence on Ethical Fund Performance and Investment Style', *Limburg Institute of Financial Economics (LIFE) Working Paper* (2002)

Bogle, John C., 'Lightning Strikes: The Creation of Vanguard, the First Index Mutual Fund, and the Revolution It Spawned', *Journal of Portfolio Management* (2014)

Chambers, David (et al), 'Keynes the Stock Market Investor: A Quantitative Analysis', *Journal of Financial and Quantitative Analysis* (2015)

De Bondt, Werner and Thaler, Richard, 'Does the Stock Market Overreact?', *Journal of Finance* (1985)

Dobretz, Wolfgang (et al), 'Corporate Governance and Expected Stock Returns: Evidence from Germany', *European Financial Management* (2004)

Gompers, Paul (et al), 'Corporate Governance and Equity Prices', *Quarterly Journal of Economics* (2003)

Hughes, Sally, 'Early Bay Area Venture Capitalists: Shaping the Economic and Business Landscape: Interview with Thomas J Perkins', *University of California Berkley Working Paper* (2009)

Jegadeesh, Narasimham and Titman, Sheridan, 'Returns to Buying Winners and Selling Losers: Implications for Stock Market Efficiency', *Journal of Finance* (1993)

Kempf, Alexander and Osthoff, Peer, 'The Effect of Socially Responsible Investing on Portfolio Performance', *Centre for Financial Research Working Paper* (2007)

Menkhoff, Lukas, 'Currency Momentum Strategies', *Journal of Financial Economics* (2012)

Philips, Christopher B. [et al], 'The Active-Passive Debate: Market Cyclicality and Leadership Volatility', *Vanguard Research Working Paper* (2014)

Samuelson, Paul, 'An Enjoyable Life Pouring over Modern Finance Theory', *Annual Review of Financial Economics* (2009)

Samuelson, Paul, 'Challenge to Judgement', *Journal of Portfolio Management* (1974)

Wallick, Daniel W. [et al], 'Keys to Improving the Odds of Active Management Success', *Vanguard Research Working Paper* (2015)

Wallick, Daniel W. [et al], 'The case for Vanguard active management: Solving the low-cost/top-talent paradox?', *Vanguard Research Working Paper* (2013)

C. Newspaper and magazine articles

Ahmed, Azam, "Soros to Close His Fund to Outsiders", *New York Times*, July 26, 2011

Authers, John, "Ed Thorp: the man who beat the casinos, then the markets", *Financial Times*, February 3, 2007

Caldwell, Kyle, "Nick Train: 'I have not bought or sold a share for four years'", *Daily Telegraph*, April 30, 2015

Cray, Douglas W., "Benjamin Graham: Securities Expert", *New York Times*, September 23, 1976

Crudele, John, "Expert Failed to Follow Instincts Before Crash", *Los Angeles Times*, December 6, 1987

Deedes, "Neil Woodford Profile: How patience and long-termism turned the Berkshire boy into the UK's top fund manager", *Daily Mail*, March 25, 2017

Evans, Judith, "Neil Woodford raises record £800m for new trust", *Financial Times*, April 20, 2015

Evans, Richard, "How Neil Woodford made you a fortune", *Daily Telegraph*, 19 October, 2013

Evans, Richard, "Neil Woodford talks: 'My best is yet to come'", *Daily Telegraph*, May 3, 2014

Gerrard, Bradley, "Anthony Bolton: 'I was wrong about the market in China'", *Financial Times*, April 13, 2014

Harvey, Daniel Whittle, "David Ricardo", *Sunday Times*, September 14, 1823

Lavites, Stuart, "Philip A. Fisher, 96, Is Dead; Wrote Key Investment Book", *New York Times*, April 19, 2004

Mackintosh, James, "Seeing the Woodford for the trees", *Financial Times*, October 15, 2013

McFadden, Robert D., "John Templeton, Investor, Dies at 95", *New York Times*, July 9, 2008

Marriage, Madison, "Nick Train: Why I'm still holding Pearson", *Financial Times*, February 25, 2017

Newlands, Chris and Marriage, Madison "99% of actively managed US equity funds underperform", *Financial Times*, October 24, 2016

Noer, Michael, "Michael Steinhardt, Wall Street's Greatest Trader, Is Back – And He's Reinventing Investing Again", *Forbes*, February 12, 2014

Peltz, James, "Funds Legend Calls It Quits, Will Cash-In Huge Portfolio", *Los Angeles Times*, October 12, 1995

Powley, Tanya, "Fund manager Woodford quits: Q&A", *Financial Times*, October 18, 2013

Schoenberger, Chana R. "Peter Lynch, 25 Years Later: It's Not Just 'Invest in What You Know'", *Wall Street Journal*, December 6, 2015

Strom, Stephanie, "Top Manager to Close Shop on Hedge Funds", *New York Times*, October 12, 1995

Tam, Pui-Wing, "Thomas J. Perkins, Pioneering Venture Capitalist in Silicon Valley, Dies at 84", *New York Times*, June 9, 2016

Train, Nick, "Six Long-Term Stalwarts to Tuck Away", *MoneyWeek*, March 11, 2016

Various, "Cotton 'King' A Bankrupt", *New York Times*, February 18, 1915

Various, "Fund Managers In a Merger", *New York Times*, November 2, 1992

Various, "Jesse Livermore Has Bodyguard, Wall Street Operator Hires Former Policeman After Threats", *New York Times*, December 21, 1929

Various, "Jesse Livermore not in Bear Pool", *New York Times*, October 22, 1929

Various, "Jesse Livermore Suspended", *New York Times*, March 8, 1934

Vartan, Vartanig G., "T. Rowe Price, 85, Growth Stock Strategist, Dead", *New York Times*, October 22, 1983

Vitello, Paul, "Robert W. Wilson, Frugal Philanthropist, Dies at 87", *New York Times*, December 27, 2013

Webb, Merryn Somerset, "Nick Train: Don't entrust your money to the clever-clogs", *MoneyWeek*, September 23, 2016

Webb, Merryn Somerset, "Why I'm not that into Warren Buffett", *Financial Times*, January 20, 2017

Weinstein, Michael M., "Paul A. Samuelson, Economist, Dies at 94", *New York Times*, December 13, 2009

D. Other sources

ANNUAL REPORTS OF:

Berkshire Hathaway
Invesco
Woodford Investment Management
Lindsell Train
Fidelity

Performance data provided by Bloomberg

THANKS

John Stepek, Cris Heaton, Ben Judge, Chris Carter, Sarah Moore and the rest of my colleagues at *MoneyWeek*. Chris Parker and the Harriman House team. Clive Moffatt. Neil Woodford, Paul Farrow and Woodford Investment Management. Roemer McPhee and Scott Lorenz. Ben Johnson and Morningstar.

INDEX

THANKS
FOR READING!

Our readers mean everything to us at Harriman House. As a special thank-you for buying this book let us help you save as much as possible on your next read:

If you've never ordered from us before, get £5 off your first order at **harriman-house.com** with this code: si5o1

Already a customer? Get £5 off an order of £25 or more with this code: 5si25

Get 7 days' FREE access to hundreds of our books at **volow.co** – simply head over and sign up.

Thanks again!
from the team at